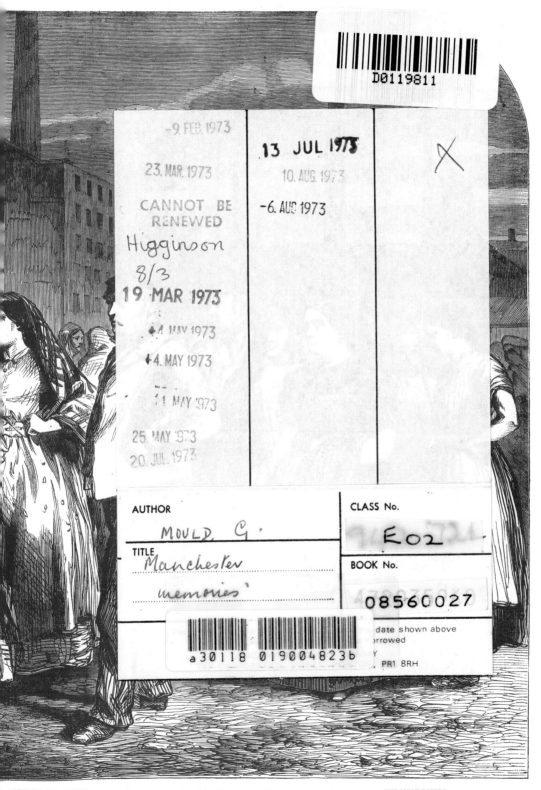

POWER-LOOM WEAVER.   SELF-ACTING MINDER. WEAVER.   THROSTLE-DOFFER.
CARDER.   POWER-LOOM WEAVER.   JACK-TENTER.
RATIVES AT MANCHESTER.

MANCHESTER MEMORIES

MANCHESTER MEMORIES

by

GEORGE MOULD

TERENCE DALTON LIMITED
LAVENHAM . SUFFOLK
1972

Published by

TERENCE DALTON LIMITED

SBN 900963 41 7

Printed in Great Britain at

THE LAVENHAM PRESS LIMITED

LAVENHAM   .   SUFFOLK

CONTENTS

		Page
Index of Illustrations		6
Acknowledgement		7
Introduction:	Why I Wrote It	8
Chapter One	We Rode in a Hansom	11
Chapter Two	The Wise Old Owl	15
Chapter Three	Do You Remember the Shambles?	27
Chapter Four	Concilio et Labore	31
Chapter Five	Backstage Interlude	37
Chapter Six	A Cedar Box	47
Chapter Seven	On the Calls	57
Chapter Eight	Clubland	63
Chapter Nine	Over the Bridges	69
Chapter Ten	Welsh Hymns and Brass Bands	79
Chapter Eleven	Reaching the Hearts of Men	85
Chapter Twelve	Twinkle Twinkle Machine	93
Chapter Thirteen	City at War	97
Chapter Fourteen	A Hole in the Head?	107
Chapter Fifteen	Manchester Alphabet	111
Chapter Sixteen	Envoi	115

INDEX OF ILLUSTRATIONS

Art Gallery	9
Albert Square	10
Barton Arcade	12
Bank building, King Street	13
Deansgate, 1895	14
Old Hanging Bridge	16
Poet's Corner	17
Laying tram tracks	18
Kitchen, Chetham's Hospital	19
Library, Chetham's Hospital	21
Cottages, Artillery Street	24
"Old Building", Grammar School	25
Old Market Place	26
Wellington Inn	28
Old Market Place	30
Albert Square, 1901	32
Rainy day, 1929	34
Library of "the humanities"	35
St Peter's Square, 1939	38
Fog, February, 1934	40
Roof top view of Manchester	41
Piccadilly, Manchester, 1890	43
Market Place and Old Shambles	44
Princes Theatre	46
Market Street, 1890	48
16 Mosley Street	49
Title page, *Manchester Herald*	51
Market Street, 1900	53
City's Reference Library, 1929	55
Blackfriars Bridge	56
Police horse	60
Police communications	61
Cross and Market Streets, 1870s	62
Albert Memorial	64
Mosley Street, 1824	65
Traffic snarl up	67
Blackfriars Street, 1890s	70
Flat Iron Market	71
Blackfriars Bridge, 1825	72
Flat Iron Market	73
Royal visit to Salford, 1851	74
Royal visitors entering Peel Park	75
Market Street, 1894	77
"The Hidden Gem"	78
Whit Week, 1938	80
St Peter's Church	81
Church of the Holy Name	83
St Ann's Square, 1866	86
Lever's Hall	87
Oldham Street, 1894	88
Smithy Door	89
Fatted Calf Hotel	90
Experts on horses	92
Heaton House, 1795	94
Belle Vue, 1908	95
"Pals" Battalions, 1915	98
Moult Street, 1912	99
Bull's Head Hotel	101
Seven Stars	102
Kersal Cell	104
Suffragettes, 1913	105
Oldham Street, 1894	106
Football buses	108
Long Millgate	110
Manchester Alphabet A to I	114-15
Manchester Alphabet J to R	120-21
Manchester Alphabet S to Z	124-25
Deansgate Arcade, 1955	128
New Cross	130
St James's Hall	131
Tib Street	132

For my wife, Anne Constance Fairlie Mould

ACKNOWLEDGEMENT

IT WOULD be difficult to over-emphasise my indebtedness and gratitude to the able chief of the Manchester Public Libraries, Mr D. I. Colley, M.A., F.L.A., for sanctioning my free access to the wonderful 80,000 strong picture collection in the Local History Library. The Local History Librarian, Mr C. E. Makepeace, was my guide and adviser in the amazing wonderland under his control.

These gentlemen made this book possible.

My gratitude also to the Chief Constable, Manchester and Salford Police who kindly supplied the photographs showing the changes in police radio communications.

Also I must acknowledge the wisdom of my parents in sending me to Manchester Grammar School in the days of Long Millgate and J. L. Paton.

Endpapers:
A group of Lancashire cotton mill operatives in 1862 when there was a "cotton famine" and workers endured privation rather than work with raw material produced by slave labour in the United States.

Why I Wrote It

RIP van Winkle had a difficult time adjusting to the changed circumstances which met him when he awoke from a rather lengthy nap. Today things change rather more rapidly. In a recent war efforts were made to change the political outlook of the people of Manchester by dropping high explosives and incendiary materials on their buildings.

The resultant clearance of property has afforded an opportunity for much rebuilding. While lofty new buildings have been towering toward the sky new road links have been shaping to keep traffic moving.

Approach Manchester by any form of transport and you may well say "this is no mean city". It is my city. I love it. Although I live no longer within its orbit it keeps its hold on my fidelity.

It shakes me, however, to think that there are generations which know the city only as it is today. It has so much history, not merely the history of centuries past but of the last century.

There must be something in the atmosphere of the area crossed by the Rivers Irwell, Irk, Medlock and Mersey. The Romans garrisoned it with the twentieth legion. It was a Legion of Friesians — not black and white cattle but Teutonic mercenaries from Friesland. There is no evidence that they ever left the shores of this island. They liked Mancunium and the rest of what is now Lancashire far too well.

The Danes liked the place and it was with difficulty that they were persuaded to leave. A mural in Manchester Town Hall records their departure.

In my day people of every clime and tongue have come to Manchester and liked it. I admire the good taste of all these settlers.

Always to me it has been an interesting city. What frightens me is that in the speed of change much of value may be lost.

I have not attempted any kind of scientific or carefully organised survey or research. So to speak I have unleashed my memory and have set down these things which it told me of. This is just one man's book of memories — not an autobiography — just memories, perhaps out of sequence but I hope none the less entertaining.

It may be that this book achieves its greatest value if it stimulates other and perhaps wiser and better informed human storehouses of memory to set down the things they recall.

Our minstrels today are not of a type to bring old Manchester to life.

Perhaps in the modern idiom I should call this book a catalyst which will I hope activate the will to record the vernacular past. I know that much has been done to put on record various chapters in Manchester's history. It would be foolish for me to suggest that the appropriate organisations have not done a first rate job.

I hope they will forgive me for thinking that my rather off-beat meanderings may find a comfortable niche.

A choice picture of the Manchester City Art Gallery.

HAPPY NEW YEAR

CHAPTER ONE

We Rode in a Hansom

DO YOU remember the toy shop in Deansgate? It was in a basement and the newel post of the staircase was a queer kind of one man band with a clown's head on top.

We rode from the *Princes Theatre* matinées to Victoria Station to catch the train home — we rode in a hansom cab and when we climbed up the high step into the cab the cabby raised his little trap door in the roof and asked "Where to?".

"Victoria Station and stop at the toy shop in Deansgate."

Indeed perhaps I was lifted into the hansom. I was very small and the step was very high from the pavement — high and quite a small metal surface on which to put your toe.

It was quite a daring thing for my mother to step down from the cab at the toy shop and go down there to buy for me a box of soldiers.

There was never any doubt about what I was to have — a box of Brittain's toy soldiers. They were good little soldiers in scarlet tunics and black helmets and carrying long rifles. I believe the box of half a dozen cost sixpence.

Nowadays it would be thought highly dangerous for people to do the things they did in those remote days. Feminine attire was cumbersome yet women climbed into traps and buggies — yes, and even scaled ladders to ride on the knife edge seats on the tops of buses!

I've been thinking I must explain why I am talking about the hansom and the toy shop. It's because those are probably my earliest Manchester memories.

It must be a little later that I remember my father's office. It was in King Street. He was an architect and how impressed I was to have pointed out to me the brass plate bearing his name at the foot of the long staircase which led to his office.

Not many lifts in those days though Manchester must have been better off than most cities because it had hydraulic pressure water mains. These were primarily to drive the presses which baled the cotton goods for export but the pressure was used also to drive lifts — sorry elevators — carrying goods and in some cases passengers.

11

Albert Square, Christmas 1953.

The progress of the hydraulic lift was slow and dignified. The first of those mad, racing contrivances, an American Electric Elevator, was the one installed at the *Grosvenor Hotel* at the Victoria Bridge Corner of Deansgate. The glass door of the lift proudly identified it as American and Electric!

There was a network of high pressure hydraulic water mains over the city and if one of them burst the result was spectacular.

The streets were paved with stone setts — better for the horses. Our hansom cab had rubber-shod wheels. You could hardly call the rubber circlet a tyre. I was always worried about those cabs. The driver sat on a perch fixed to the back of the passenger compartment.

The whole tendency seemed to be for the whole contrivance to lift the horse off its feet and tip the cabby off his perch. Indeed it was not unknown for one of those drivers' perches to come adrift. The reins were of extreme length — right up over the roof of the cab. The passengers were shut in behind two flap half doors. In the later cabs there was glass in the top half of the doors.

I was taken to the matinée at the *Princes Theatre*. My father was retained as the theatre architect. This was the period when Robert Courtneidge was Manager there. That most versatile comedy actress Cecily Courtneidge made her

Barton Arcade—a lovely example of Victorian use of ironwork.

A Manchester treasure—the bank building in King Street in 1939. It is much the same today.

debut at the *Princes* as Peaseblossom in *A Midsummer Night's Dream.* She was tiny then and must have been more than charming.

The show I most remember from this misty past of childhood is my first pantomime. It was *Cinderella.* The theme song was *I'll be Your Sweetheart.* Now you can date it. That was the theme song that year.

Dear old *Princes!* Trays of tea at the matinee interval — antimacassars everywhere — programme girls in decorous black and with white aprons.

Later on I want to write a whole piece about theatres but it will be about the theatres when I began to penetrate behind the scenes to interview impresarios and stars.

Just now I'm back among the gaslights — without incandescent mantles — the hansom cabs — the horse trams and horse-drawn vehicles generally — a Manchester of shadowy byways between tall warehouses, not much different from the Manchester which fascinated Charles Dickens and inspired him to write *The Christmas Carol.*

It was a noisy Manchester because horses and horse-drawn vehicles on stone paved streets were noisy. Yes, and it smelled of horses. The men wore high starched collars — not turnover collars — and heavy coats — swallow-tailed if you were a big shot in Manchester on market days.

Our cab brings us to Victoria Station. The station was only half as big as it is today. Our horse walked up Hunts Bank which was the main approach. At the top of the hill was a rather elaborate horse trough across a corner. The only platforms of that day were reached by the subway — still healthy and useful — and that subway was an adventure, particularly if a train went rumbling over our heads.

Victoria, like other stations, smelled of railway gas. Compartments — no corridors — were lit by gas which was put into containers beneath the coaches and which was 'retorted' by railway companies without the filtering refinements of municipal gas. At least judging by the smell that was the case.

Change was on the way. Victoria was to have ten new platforms. The hansoms and the growlers were to be supplanted by the internal combustion engine.

In the interim of change — which of course is continuous — came the era of the bicycle during which cyclists were fined for scorching — literally for riding too fast!

Suburban newsboys took to bicycles like ducks to water.

And I was growing up.

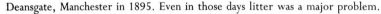

Deansgate, Manchester in 1895. Even in those days litter was a major problem.

CHAPTER TWO

The Wise Old Owl

I WAS growing up. This is not a signal that I am launched on an autobiography. If I begin to drift that way I hope someone is around to stop me. I have started this piece of writing because I want to put on record while it is still in my memory, the portrait of a city I love.

It is very easy to love Manchester. There may be those who laugh at the idea. There are those who think that the country north of Watford is a jungle the inhabitants of which dress in woad and speak in strange tongues.

I love Manchester and I've known many other people who loved it. It isn't just because I'm ignorant of other cities. I've surprised a few Londoners by showing them an off beat London they'd never heard of! I'm very fond of London and Dublin and Edinburgh.

But I love Manchester.

After my toy shop days I next met the city when it was decided to send me to Manchester Grammar School. At the ripe age of eleven I started to travel every day by train a distance of nine miles to school. I wore a little dark blue cap with light blue circumferal stripes and a silver owl badge on its front. Life became a great adventure.

In those days the school had a total of boys running into four figures. The High Master was J. L. Paton. It was said that he could identify every boy in the school by name. Certainly he never failed to identify me by name.

It is thought that we who were at the school in J. L. Paton's day believe that never before or since has the school been so great. Graduates of later regimes accept this school of thought with amused tolerance. Indeed, I have heard a later High Master make witty apology to a gathering of veteran Old Boys because his name was not J. L. Paton.

However, all this may be, I think it is true that in my time at the school it was very much a part of the life of the centre of the city. It would have been strange if boys did not manage to get around in their forty-five minute luncheon break.

School was a great adventure.

The old Hanging Bridge near the Cathedral photographed when it was excavated and restored in the early years of the century.

The building we knew as the "old building" is still there in Long Millgate.

The period of my Manchester schooling was the period of the city's greatness as capital of the cotton textile industry. It was a very cosmopolitan city. Merchants from many countries were established in the city.

It was said that an incomer from overseas could make a fortune dealing in what native Manchester threw away. There were boys of many creeds at the school and one soon learned that many of them were as handy with their fists as anyone with Lancashire roots.

The area best known to us was of course that most adjacent to the school. We were conscious of the immediate proximity of Chetham's Hospital, the blue-coat school founded to educate the sons of "poor but industrious parents". We felt that Humphrey Chetham had a worthy charitable aim — oblivious of the fact that Hugh Oldham, Bishop of Exeter had exactly the same intention when he founded the grammar school — indeed that the *real* grammar school boys were those holding foundation scholarships!

Being incurably inquisitive I explored Chetham's and found that I was not questioned if I climbed the stairs to the corner where Harrison Ainsworth wrote novels and where Karl Marx sat collating his material for *Das Kapital*.

16

The discovery gave me a great idea. By having a hurried lunch I could have time to creep into Chetham's and do my homework for the afternoon classes. Needless to say there came a day when authority spotted what I was up to and I had to change my ways.

Across from our new building in those days was Poets' Corner, a very ancient building, the ground floor of which was a tuck shop. There were various theories as to why the old building was called Poets' Corner. Its upstairs bulged over the pavement. Perhaps it was decrepit and they pulled it down to save its life. Anyway it disappeared.

A little further round were the offices and plant of the Co-operative Press and by looking through ground floor windows we could see presses and folding and stapling machines at work.

Not far away was the Collegiate School. The boys wore Eton suits and sang in the Cathedral Choir.

Our view was that they were "bumstarved". It was believed that their neat little stone building was riddled with dry rot and it was sold as unfit for modern teaching. It stands today and houses among other activities a florists' shop and a restaurant.

It wasn't far to the Produce Exchange and other buildings in the basements of which were cheese and bacon warehouses. The smell of large quantities of cheese and bacon is not easily forgotten. Some of those cool below-ground warehouses still do duty.

Poet's Corner, Long Millgate, as an antique store. The date of this picture is not known.

The laying of the track for the electric tramway cars, corner of St Mary's Gate and Victoria Street, 1901.

There were various places where a boy could have lunch. There was of course an official school lunch with the High Master at the top table and staff on each side of him.

In the basement of the school was "Lizzie's". We called her Lizzie and she was very competent in dealing with noisy, hungry boys.

Lizzie stood in the centre of a square of sweet stalls. At the hour of our lunch break there was delivered to her a large container of what was described as hot pot but which was really meat and potato hash. For twopence one could have a very large plate of this dish. I can't say that the digestion of it conduced to wakefulness in the afternoon.

There were odd things like meat pies (twopence each) at Poets Corner. In Corporation Street was a small but very well run restaurant called *Robertson's*. Miss Robertson was a very attractive person with very lovely auburn hair. On those occasions when we lunched at *Robertson's* we looked at her as at a goddess. I believe she was not long unmarried.

One could have sausages and mashed potatoes for sixpence — a goodly helping — I think Miss Robertson saw that we were given plenty of filling. One day I arrived there to find to my horror that I'd lost my lunch money. She gave me a scolding glance and then said "Don't worry. Pay me tomorrow."

In a building which still exists in Withy Grove was a three or four storey restaurant called *Gradwell's*. It was an area of robust living — cut off the joint and "three veg". Superior clerks and warehouse people lunched there with gusto which could be observed from the street.

In Market Street was *The Ceylon* — the restaurant of the Ceylon Tea Company — which was elegant and had music — a small orchestra — and a smoke room floor. Later it became a Lyons tea place and now it has disappeared.

But boys couldn't get too far away from the school. The afternoon session was short — we finished at 3.10 p.m. because so many boys had train journeys home.

The Cathedral of course was our church. We had a Founder's Day service there. Can you imagine the squeaking of wooden chairs on hard stone floors with a congregation of fidgetty small boys? In those days I wondered why a Bishop of Exeter should be interested in founding a school in Lancashire. But then of course he was a scion of the Oldham family whose name associates with the town of that name. Oldham was not much of a place in his days, particularly ecclesiastically. Its place of worship was a chapel of ease under the control of the Parish of Prestwich. But the badge of the Bishop and the school and the town has been the owl.

The great kitchen of Chetham's Hospital photographed in 1939 when it was still entirely a Bluecoat School where the boys were boarders. To-day it has expanded and specialises in musical training.

The College of Heralds love a pun, and here is one. Natives of Oldham pronounce the name Ow'dham or Owldem — and they are right! That must have been the ancient pronunciation.

If you have a chance to look at Hugh Oldham's tomb in Exeter Cathedral you will find that it has all its ancient colour and in every possible space is an owl.

The chap we recognised most readily was of course Humphrey Chetham whose effigy still sits in the Cathedral. And with his back to the Cathedral outside stood Oliver Cromwell.

There was an occasion when King Edward VII and Queen Alexandra visited Manchester. They arrived by train, at Exchange Station, and drove in an open carriage to the Town Hall. The carriage was drawn by greys.

An enormous wooden stand was erected to accommodate Grammar School boys. It was a wonderful vantage point. We were marshalled to our seats well in advance of the Royal arrival and there was not a seat vacant. It was years before I realised that buried beneath the load of boys was — Oliver Cromwell!

History says that it was because of the existence of that statue that Queen Victoria refused to open the present Manchester Town Hall. The Lord Mayor of the day carried out the opening ceremony himself on what was recorded as the wettest day in living memory.

Cromwell has been moved. Did you know that in the area where he used to stand and right along between the Cathedral and the River Irwell is a street which was put underground — under arches — when the improved embankment was created — shops, lampposts etc., — all gone underground.

I can just remember a little steamer plying on the Irwell from landing stages near Victoria Bridge.

Mention of the bridge reminds me that it was because the Civil War started here that Cromwell was sited nearby.

Manchester was noisy in the period I am writing of. Lorries were noisy, steel-shod wheels on granite setts. J. L. Paton drew our attention to the fact that the empty ones made the biggest noise. The trams were noisy, horse-drawn until about 1901.

And there was a practice which was very noisy. It was usual to back a flat lorry up to the wall beneath a doorway or window on an upper floor of a warehouse. 'Lumps' of cloth — rolls in other words — were dropped from these upper storeys onto the lorry. They were dropped with great precision so that they didn't hit the lorry driver who was doing the packing. But what a noise they made on impact! What they did to the lorry springs was nobody's business.

The fireplace end of the Reading Room of the Library at Chetham's Hospital, Manchester. Here Harrison Ainsworth wrote novels and Karl Marx assembled information and ideas.

Then news vendors were much more noisy than they are today. There was fierce competition between the two evening papers. And along the kerb in Market Street were salesmen offering penny toys made in Germany or Japan. They described their wares loudly to the passers by. They were safe if they kept on the move, shuffling continually along the kerb, but if they stood still they could be prosecuted.

It was during these Grammar School days that I first made contact with the Free Trade Hall. I put it that way for a reason which will emerge. Once a year we went to the Free Trade Hall for Speech Day, a great occasion at which parents were present and had the opportunity of being proud of their sons if their sons had done anything to be proud of.

We had a preliminary run through which enabled us to find our places in the hall with discipline and good order. There *were* speeches and we sang. Once it was *Land of Hope and Glory.* On other occasions we sang *Gaudeamus Igitur* and *Die Lorelei.* Versatile we were.

It was after one of the rehearsals that some of us hid so that we got left behind in the hall. We wanted to explore. It was such a ponderous Victorian magnificence. It was decorated chiefly in pastel shades of blue.

At the back of the hall facing the stage was a row of boxes — like very big theatre boxes. Later in life I occupied one of them officially at a big engineering occasion. To us boys they were a temptation and an invitation. We worked out that with some careful scaling one could climb the pillars and get into one of those boxes.

Now we were alone in the hall and we were going to try it. I was nearly there, just negotiating a slight bulge in the apron of the box when a stern voice from below said "Come down". I risked a peep and there were my pals looking very pale and anxious and there was a burly chap, evidently a member of the staff of the Free Trade Hall.

I wondered what to do. Should I keep on up and risk dodging capture? The voice from below made it clear that if I got into the box I should find the door locked. No exit except by the way I had entered.

Carefully I reluctantly descended. From his subsequent remarks I gathered that my captor was chiefly concerned about (a) any damage I might do to the paintwork and (b) any damage I might do to myself. I also gathered that he spoke more in sorrow than in anger and that somewhere in his career he had been a boy himself.

He let me go.

That old hall was gutted by enemy action in the Second World War, and I was sorry because I felt that I had special knowledge of its architecture — a special contact with it.

What else about my schoolday memories of Manchester? Well, of course, Withy Grove was always a near-at-hand centre of interest. Two old pubs gave it olde worlde atmosphere — the *Seven Stars* and the *Rover's Return*. The *Seven Stars* really was very old — one of the oldest taverns in the country. Of course we never saw the inside of them. They're gone now.

There were book barrows and there was the "Quack Market". This market had no connection with bogus medicine. It was a poultry market. Maybe a shadow of it still exists. Living hens were offered for sale and it was queer to hear them clucking in a city street.

And Victoria Station! They were building the new platforms — one to ten. One day we were marched out to platform one and there far below us we saw the River Irk. There *is* a Grammar School song which makes reference to "the clear running stream of the Irk". By the time I got a look at it, it was far from clear running. And they were about to cover it over with railway station. That was why the Railway Company had offered us an opportunity of seeing "our" river.

Oh yes, there were railway companies in those days. The prettiest trains were the occasional ones into Manchester belonging to the Furness Railway. They were painted in attractive shades of blue and the locomotives were highly polished and had much brass.

The North Staffordshire Railway running into London Road had a Staffordshire knot as its symbol. The compartments on the Great Central were pleasantly decorative — pictures and mirrors.

Of course, Victoria was Lancashire and Yorkshire having recently absorbed the East Lancashire Railway. Exchange was London and North Western and into Central came Midland, Cheshire Lines Committee and Manchester Altrincham and South Junction trains. Some Cambrian stock found its way to Manchester.

Piccadilly? I just remember the old Infirmary with its centre dome. In front were sunken gardens which had once been claypits with a pond where scolds were ducked.

There was a two-wheeled hand ambulance kept in a kind of cubby hole in a wall with an easily opened door. A policeman or helpful stranger could wheel it out and take it to the spot where someone had collapsed or met with an accident. It was just a stretcher on wheels.

Near at hand, where it is today, is the central Fire Station which we were taken to visit. We were allowed to slide down poles from floor to floor as the firemen did

Survival! Cottages in Artillery Street not too far from the City centre.

when an alarm bell rang and we saw the winged collars and hinged harness fall onto the necks of the wonderfully trained horses. Oh yes, there were some very heavy motorised units but to us the horses were the thrill.

And now I must tell you about my introduction to the world of politics. One lunch time near the school we saw a crowd and presently an open landau drew up and a very elegant young man stepped out. He wore complete morning dress, striped trousers, swallow-tailed coat, silk topper and spats. I was told that he was Mr. Winston Churchill campaigning because he was standing as candidate for a local constituency. Of course he was accompanied by his agent and other local worthies.

He was about to approach the crowd with a smile and a handshake, I suppose, when he was assailed by a shower of noisome missiles. They were thrown by women wearing the traditional Lancashire clogs and shawl. I was told that these were carters' wives. In those days the carters — horse-lorry drivers — were Manchester's militant spearhead.

The conveying of cotton goods from warehouse to ship or to railway was an operation vital to the city's life blood. For some reason the carter fraternity didn't like Mr. Churchill. The women growled and shouted abuse. Mr. Churchill addressed the crowd briefly and with such calmness and penetration as was possible. Then he got back into his landau and drove away.

The missiles which had been hurled at him had fortunately missed. Schoolboy curiosity sent us to investigate. The women had thrown "bombs" created by wrapping rotten fruit and tomatoes and other gutter scrapings from the Shudehill fruit market in lengths of old newspaper.

Well, I was still growing up, and Manchester was doing what it has done persistently and in common with other towns. It was altering.

The entrance to the "Old Building" of Manchester Grammar School. The "New Building" was destroyed in the Second World War. The school left Millgate before the war.

CHAPTER THREE

Do You Remember the Shambles?

ONCE upon a time there was an area surviving right in the centre of Manchester which was a joy to the lover of ancient places and a trial and anxiety to the police and other authorities.

It was known to most people under the general name of "The Shambles" although that was really the name of only a small part of it. It was better described by an even older generation as "The Old Market Place". I can remember that on Market days, Tuesdays and Fridays, there could be a few stalls in its widest area.

It was a warren of narrow streets in which was an amazing collection of licensed premises. Best known perhaps was the *Bull's Head* which housed a curious three cornered chair in which it was said Prince Charles had sat when he made his headquarters there when he reached Manchester during the 1745 rebellion. There was the *Falstaff* and the *Black Bull* and the *Wellington* and the *Slip Inn* and even then I don't think I'm naming them all.

Most of them supplied sandwiches, some of them supplied luncheon. At midday they were respectable enough — merchants from the Royal Exchange across the way crowded into them. At night they attracted a very mixed crowd. The narrow passage ways were an attraction to some pretty sleazy customers and many a cotton man delaying his homeward journey for a "quick one" stayed longer than he should and came round to find himself with a hangover and no wallet!

The shops in the area were a joy. There was one which specialized in vintage China teas. There was an ancient underground skittle alley where rare cheeses were stored. There were kippers and fresh salmon and trout, and hand-raised pies and game in season and Bath chaps and sweetbreads and hams of rare curing — some delicious black ham — and Bury puddings, and all the things that tempt the palate of the homegoing male.

My father returning from his Manchester office might have a neat little parcel of some special treat. It was often doubtful whether the family shared his rare taste for exotic foods. My own special joy was Lancashire sage cheese.

Hitler's airborne representatives wiped out the Old Market Place in one night. The only survival is the oldest building of the lot — the *Wellington*, built

The Old Market Place in the late 90s showing on the left the lamp above the entrance to the underground shooting range and skittle alley which later became a cheese store. Hitler and demolition experts have cleared away nearly all these buildings.

The *Wellington Inn* was once the home of John Bryom, who wrote "Christians Awake", seen here in 1958 before underground car parks were created in the foreground. Now, at the time of writing, the whole block is to be raised six feet.

in 1328 and now carefully preserved and raised on a concrete base — a brilliant feat of engineering. It lived through a night of bombing because it had stood so much — so many changes and vicissitudes — that nothing could daunt it.

The oldest pictures of it I have seen show it with a huge pair of wooden spectacles decorating its frontage. Presumably it was then the headquarters of an optician. It was once the home of John Byrom who invented a system of shorthand, which he taught, played the organ at Manchester "Old Church", now the Cathedral, and wrote the hymn *Christians Awake* which the whole wide world sings.

More recently it has housed a philatelist and a numismatist, well I suppose they collected because they offered stamps and coins for sale. Also I believe there was an antique sales corner.

On the morning after the destruction of the Old Market Place and its environs a fellow journalist came into my office in search of sympathy.

He had done a tour of inspection of the desolation.

"All those beautiful pubs gone in one night, George" he said. "It's nothing short of disaster!"

Talking about the Old Market Place and the Shambles reminds me of the Pack Drill Club. How it earned its name I never discovered. It was a loosely organised fellowship of men chiefly but not exclusively engaged in journalistic pursuits. There was no entrance or membership fee or initiation ceremony.

The formula was that a member decided that he had found a catering establishment which could provide some regional dish. Each member would receive a summons in due legal form on blue paper ordering his presence to help to adjudicate on the authenticity of the dish. After the consumption of the meal, the chairman of the evening would don wig and gown and sit in judgement on the dish. The opinions of those who had eaten it were heard. If it was found that the dish as offered had lacked authenticity then the rule was that the member who had proposed and ordered it should pay the bill for the occasion.

The rule was never enforced though it was never found that the meal was beyond criticism. It was great fun. Outstanding evenings which I remember were one at which we ate a Barnsley chop and another at an Armenian restaurant, the *Ararat*, when we ate kebabs and an amazing sweet made from rose petals.

On one occasion all the 'evidence' was given in verse of greater or less merit.

The occasion I am remembering which brings me back to the Old Market Place was a meeting at the *Black Bull*.

The dish of the evening was a Lancashire hot pot. There are some pretty sordid ideas in some places as to what a real Lancashire hot pot should be like. It isn't just the hash of chopped potatoes and bits of meat which carries the title in some places. It is a dish of noble character for robust palates and powerful digestions. It has much more character than lobscouse but then Merseyside has its own palate and must be listened to with respect. And Merseyside folk don't think of themselves as Lancashire folk.

Hot pot grows in a large earthenware dish. The bottom is covered with sliced potato on top of which is a layer consisting of cutlets from best end of neck or lamb chops garnished with slices of sheeps' kidneys and oysters. On top of this is a crust of chopped potatoes which is heavily buttered so that it will brown nicely. The whole should be lubricated with a rich gravy.

We had a gay and memorable evening with our Pack Drill hot pot and then agreed almost unanimously that the oysters were not oysters. The cook had substituted mussels! There was only one dissentient voice of course — the voice of the instigator of the feast.

Another feature of the area we are talking about was its display of fish, poultry and game, and everything was in prime condition. Rather than store anything at least one shopkeeper held a late Saturday afternoon 'auction' of his wares. For a shilling you could buy a mystery parcel which you might find contained some choice salmon steaks, a trout, some cod or halibut or herrings or haddock — always far far more than a shilling's worth of good food.

The custom was a great boon to some of the not so wealthy citizens. It was not exactly a pig that they bought in a poke but they knew they would never be let down — indeed in "Dutch auction" terms they often saw what went into the parcel.

What stands today where once men feasted and drank deep? Tall modern buildings and an underground and sub-underground car park. Lingering on at the moment of writing, the old *Wellington* building and Sinclairs' pie and oyster bar.

A very old picture of the Old Market Place. On the right is the Royal Exchange of the period.

CHAPTER FOUR

Concilio et Labore

AFTER that frolic around the Old Market Place I remind myself that this is a portrait of a city — not an autobiography — and turn to a look at the dignity of the city. What better place to start than the Town Hall.

My guide book tells me it is "an excellent example of the Gothic Renaissance style of architecture . . . built in 1877. The walls of the Public Room are decorated with murals by Ford Madox Brown which depict events of local historical interest".

I'll tell you a secret about those murals. The artist had filled almost all the panels on one side of the hall by actually painting on the wall when it was realised that this could be a mistake. The rest of the panels were painted on canvas stretched to fit the available space.

On top of the tower of the Town Hall is a huge gilt ball decorated with spikes. Early in the life of the building a pigeon impaled itself on one of the spikes and lost its life. Its remains duly taxidermed were mounted on a replica of the big metal ball and stood in the window of the Sculpture Hall of the building for many years.

There was once a newspaper fuss about a bust of William Shakespeare in the Sculpture Hall. Someone discovered that far from being a piece of sculpture it was a piece of plaster. It was suggested that it was neither valuable nor worthy of esteem. Perhaps it had been forgotten that a masterpiece can be carved in cheese.

When the Duke of Bridgewater asked official sanction for the cutting of his canal between Manchester and Liverpool, his engineer Brindley who was a genius, though illiterate, took along a model of the bridge he would build to carry the canal over the River Mersey. His model was carved from a cheese!

Today Brindley's canal crosses the Manchester Ship Canal 'in' or 'on' a swing bridge!

I may find time to take you to the Ship Canal before I finish writing but now let us get back to the Town Hall. Many a time I've described its wonders to overseas visitors.

In the vestibule of the main entrance is tiled flooring to a pattern found in the remains of Roman Mancunium and the dark brown tiles I am told are Roman tiles.

The scene in Albert Square, Manchester in 1901 when the proclamation of the succession to the throne of Edward VII was read to the citizens from the Town Hall steps.

Beside the tiles there is a statue of Joule who invented the jacquard system of weaving. He is seen seated and pondering over a piece of mechanism which he holds in his hand. The irreverent have described this effigy as "the statue of a man with a mouse trap". Still, it is a very lifelike piece of sculpture.

Facing Joule is a statue of Dalton the scientist who made many great discoveries and did not a little towards the development of the atomic theory.

In his later years he had a meagre existence until Queen Victoria saw to it that he received a small pension. But Manchester gave him a magnificent funeral; a commemorative statue and a street named after him. Traditionally John Dalton Street is a street of bookshops.

I've wandered from the Town Hall again. I think it is a lovely old building. In 1977 it will be a hundred years old. It has some lovable features. One of them is the suite dedicated to the reigning Lord Mayor and his secretariat. You step from the corridor into a haven of decorous peace. On the ground floor of the suite, which is on the first floor of the building, you find a waiting room, a secretarial office and the Lord Mayor's Office with a dressing room beyond where he can don his robes.

On the next floor is a suite where a fair sized luncheon party can be entertained. Above this is a residential flat where a Lord Mayor can live in great comfort during his term of office.

I suppose I've seen more than my share of the comfort and hospitality of the Town Hall. For more than twenty years it was my privilege to take many 'Very Important Persons', chiefly from overseas, to be received and entertained by Lord Mayors.

Sometimes as on Royal occasions, when my duty was as custodian of the Press, the hospitality was on a lavish scale — a guest list of hundreds. Much more often we lunched very comfortably in the Lord Mayor's suite. I remember Lord Mayor Hill whose life work had been to give Manchester and Lancashire a wonderful string of restaurants and whose term of office fell in war years, saying to me thoughtfully, "Well Mould, we've eaten our way through a wonderful asparagus crop."

As might be expected he had special knowledge of the requirements of good catering. He broke no rules but his wartime hospitality to my guests was of a very high order. Asparagus was something we could have without transgressing and Town Hall preparation did it full justice.

Another story of this great Lord Mayor — he heard that the American Red Cross organisation had managed to obtain a big and very special refrigerator for their hostel in what had been previously the Conservative Club in the heart of Manchester.

He rose from his office desk and without waiting for Lord Mayoral hat, coat or motor car, strode through the streets and calling the hostel staff round him delivered a lecture on the careful and proper use of that refrigerator. It was a wonderful mechanism and he refused to allow a risk of it being misused. The Americans were delighted. "This," they said "is democracy".

The occasion was only matched by another American hostel visit when Lord Shawcross, who was then Regional Commissioner for the North West, amazed and thrilled his transatlantic audience by reciting Lincoln's Gettysburgh address.

There I go hopping around again. The subject is Manchester Town Hall with special reference to Lord Mayors. I first began to meet them across a table groaning with good fare in the early 1930s. In those days a retiring Lord Mayor thanked the Press by giving a dinner party to a chosen list of those who had written about events during his year of office — "the Town Hall gang" as someone once irreverently said.

At the first such dinner party I attended I found myself placed at table next to a *Manchester Guardian* representative called Howard Spring. Not that Howard Spring haunted the Town Hall. He was present that evening as representing the Editor of the *Manchester Guardian* who of course was busy editing. He was a very pleasant dinner table companion and it seemed that I had an aptitude for meeting him in "places where they eat".

In the past Manchester has had an utterly unjustified reputation as a rainy city. It did rain one day in 1929 and this is what it looked like. It was this day which launched the myth—perhaps!

Another occasion was in an underground restaurant called the *Squirrel*. It was run by a German interior decorator who had been interned during the war — a panic step if ever there was one for he was a peace-loving individual who had enjoyed living and working in England.

He had the idea that Manchester people might enjoy authentic German cooking — and he was right. The *Squirrel* introduced me to the true enjoyment of a Wiener Schnitzel garni.

There I met Howard Spring who admired the venture and the courage of the restaurateur.

The Town Hall — to return to its architecture — is built on a triangular site which I am told was once the 'town's yard' of the new borough of Manchester. There was once a newspaper reporter who believed in motor cycle journalism. He wasn't the first to think that a man on a powerful machine could reach the scene of an unexpected happening of any kind much faster than most people. He owned a motor cycle the vintage of which I know not but it was believed that the machine was powerful and fast.

He was challenged by a colleague to ride round the Town Hall at midnight while the great clock in the tower struck twelve.

He set out to do it one calm and peaceful midnight.

In those days city police headquarters were in the very centre of the Town Hall building and of course were manned twenty-four hours a day. As the clock sounded its first ponderous stroke the crash and roar of the push-off of a big motor cycle broke the calm of central Manchester. I don't know whether the intrepid cyclist beat the clock but certainly he found the police waiting for him at the 'finishing line'. I wasn't there. It may be that the story is in part apocryphal. It isn't a stunt which could get anywhere today.

In the days I am thinking back to big Lord Mayoral occasions were often in November when the Manchester weather could do anything except run to a heatwave. There could be fog and snow and ice. These are facts well known to those who remember the Manchester November Handicap race meeting on the course in the fold of the River Irwell.

I recall this because a thoughtful Lord Mayor would arrange for hot soup to be served to departing guests. A trolley bearing a vast tureen and many bowls and

One of the three great libraries of "the humanities" of the world today—the John Rylands Library in Deansgate, Manchester.

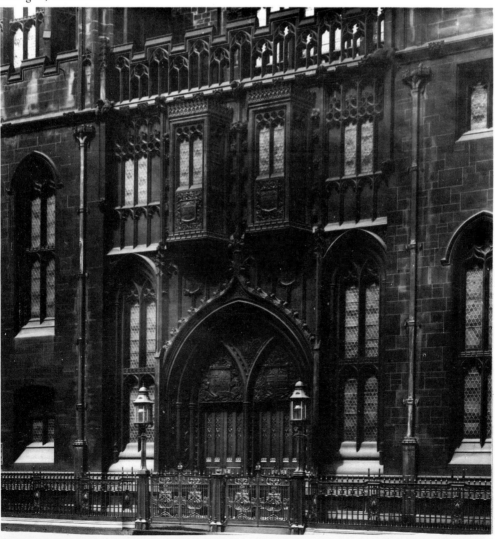

spoons and table napkins of paper would be wheeled to a point near the spot where guests were filing up to shake hands with His Lordship and the Lady Mayoress and to thank them for a delightful evening. Being much averse to cold weather, provision of that hot soup made a great impression on me.

Eventually the city fathers realised that November is not the best of months for main functions and the periodicity of the Lord Mayoral term of office was adapted to suit the Lancashire climate.

I have met many Lord Mayors — Manchester never has bad ones. Some made outstanding impressions. Of course a great deal of opportunity for a Lord Mayor to shine arises from circumstances outside Town Hall control. The Fates take a hand.

However, it may be fair to remember the amazing year of Alderman Joseph Toole. He was fond of telling people that he had started his working life as a barefoot newspaper boy in the streets of Salford. He was a Character with a capital C. Never mind his politics — Lord Mayors don't have any — he made so great an impression that there was talk of asking him to take another year of office. One could recall many stories of the reign of Joe Toole — and of course of the terms of other more orthodox worthies. But that is just one big reason why I should never have started to write this book. I mustn't tell tales out of school.

There is one story I must tell. Lord Mayors of Manchester are "Right Worshipful".

Lord Mayors of London and York are Right Honourable. I believe it was the Lord Mayoral secretariat in Manchester which drew national attention to the fact that only in the two ancient cities is the Lord Mayor ex officio a Privy Councillor and therefore entitled to the prefix Right Honourable.

It was officially confirmed that Manchester is right to call its Lord Mayor the Right Worshipful. A 'local peculiar' perhaps like calling the civic head-quarters a Town Hall — not a City Hall! And there was an occasion when the Lord Mayor's suite was a Royal Residence — when before coming to the throne King George VI and Queen Elizabeth as Duke and Duchess of York paid a visit and slept there.

CHAPTER FIVE

Backstage Interlude

WHEN I was very young my father brought home one evening a 'twopence coloured' card printed with the parts to be cut out and pasted up into a model theatre. He spent many evenings with me erecting the toy and enjoyed the job at least as much as I did.

His enthusiasm infected me and I have never been able to clear the infection from my blood. Not that I have ever wanted to. It has given me many lovely and exciting experiences on both sides of the footlights. Not that I ever became an actor — or would have liked to. It never took me that way. My pleasure was in knowing the people of the theatre and enjoying their company. It is true that twice I have strayed away to write for the stage. My playwriting is entirely episodic — plain journalism and not dramatic art. I shall tell you about those ventures briefly.

When I was old enough to have a Saturday penny I found a shop where I could buy 'penny plain' sets for pasting up and cutting out the scenery and characters for a number of plays. These sets were printed by a firm called Clark's in Manchester and the plates must be worth a fortune now if they can be found.

I created for myself a library of these plays. Some of the plates were getting worn so that the actors' script was not all too legible. But I managed with a little invention. My problem was to round up an audience. When I decided to have a session with my toy theatre I planted posters — my very own handiwork — at vantage points in the house.

Those posters were the signal for members of the household to be going out on important business or to have tasks at home which could not be left. My performances must have been incredibly boring to watch. The characters were so static, the voices so similar and the lighting so bad. On one occasion I simulated a lightning storm and set the scenery on fire.

I'm saying that I never acted but I am reminded that in a Sunday School production of "Bardell versus Pickwick" I was Mrs. Bardell's miserable child. All I had to do was to be noisy in the right places — no spoken part.

Before this develops any further into a slice of my own history let me tell you how it ties up with my picture of a bygone Manchester. After I came reporting

Bird's eye view of St Peter's Square in 1939. Most of the buildings in the immediate background, including the *Princes Theatre*, have disappeared.

around in Manchester and Salford I had one or two inevitable assignments to interview celebrities of the stage. Very early in my experience I met film star Florence Turner. She came to England and to Lancashire to appear as a mill girl!

I was very callow and deeply impressed.

Years later when Edgar Wallace was launching one of his plays in Manchester I interviewed him in his suite at the Midland Hotel. It was late morning and he was pacing around in a very becoming dressing gown. He was washed and shaved and breakfasted of course.

"How much space have you got to fill?" he asked.

"Two thirds of a column," I said.

"Take this," he said and dictated without hesitation a grand interview which when I typed it filled two thirds of a column exactly!

In the early 1920s I graduated to a national morning paper and stayed there for some ten years. It was invaluable experience. It gave me my introduction to the real world of the theatre in Manchester and to the city's police world which I shall tell you about in another chapter.

I had opportunity to do some research and concluded that Manchester has always been able to support three theatres of various kinds. There have been times when there were many more particularly in the suburbs but those in the centre of the city have been a kind of backbone establishment.

Do you remember the *Broadheads*? They were built by a theatre enthusiast, W. H. Broadhead, who took special interest in the actual bricks and mortar of his circuit. It was said that when he built a new theatre he actually knew the current price of bricks and timber. His places were chiefly music halls but he had one or two theatres built for melodrama. The Play House complex in Hulme where the B.B.C. pioneered much northern television and where they do much sound radio recording was the heart and centre of the Broadhead circuit.

They were rollicking places catering for the densely populated inner suburbs. The Broadheads gave George Formby junior the chance to develop his act. After his father died he tried to follow his pattern but it was not a success. It was when he took to the ukulele and a style of his own that he really found favour and popularity.

The 'in town' theatres I remember were the *Theatre Royal, The Princes,* the *Opera House,* the *Gaiety,* the *Tivoli,* the *Palace* and the *Hippodrome.*

Probably the one most written and talked about was the *Gaiety* because it housed Miss Horniman's launching of the Repertory movement. It had been the

"Night must fall". On 12th February 1934 fog came down on Piccadilly, Manchester. This was what it looked like. No wonder Manchester pioneered in creating a smokeless zone in the city centre. We don't get such fogs now.

Folly theatre and its peculiarity was that it was half below ground level. When you entered the theatre you were on the level of the dress circle. I remember that Miss Horniman would sit in the stage box smoking a dark cheroot and watching the show critically.

She would only allow a show to run for a week and she was very angry when after a brief absence from Manchester she found arrangements in hand to run *Hindle Wakes* for a second week. It was taken off and other people put it on tour where it ran for years and years and years. On their posters was the publicity slogan "Hindle Wakes never sleeps".

The *Theatre Royal* was one of the old theatres Royal having a royal licence legitimizing them. I have been told that as long as there was music the bar could stay open. Enterprising drinkers would pay one of the violinists in the orchestra to go on playing long after the show ended.

The facade of the *Theatre Royal* before alteration was very beautiful — very dignified.

The *Opera House* started life as the *New Queen's Theatre* which was changed to the *New Theatre* which then became *Opera House*. It was built to replace the

Queen's Theatre which had stood where the Masonic Temple stands now in Bridge Street.

It was built for a Manager called Flanagan who specialised in spectacular Shakespearean productions. Of course he did not go much for Kings and Queens. He wanted *As You Like It* or *Midsummer Night's Dream* or *Merry Wives of Windsor,* the truth being that if there was a forest it must be a forest and there must be live sheep and rabbits. Without a babbling rivulet and a deer or two the show was not up to standard.

I don't remember Flanagan's Shakespeare but I do remember the same kind of Shakespearean production at the *Hippodrome.*

There it could be done very well. The stage could be retracted revealing a circus ring, hence *Hippodrome.* The floor of the ring could be lowered so that water flowed in and a water spectacle could be put on. Thus it will be seen it was comparatively simple to have plenty of water flowing around and plenty of room for 'real' grassy mounds with living animals.

What the pigeon sees. Recent roof top view of Manchester with Cathedral in the foreground.

The Palace was for long the home of the top rankers in Music Hall entertainment. It graduated by way of big band shows to sophisticated revue — Charlot, Cochran, Coward — and eventually to the West End spectaculars.

The *Opera House* brought grand opera, ballet, Shakespeare. Of course I'm not suggesting that they never crossed each other's paths.

I saw Cochran revue produced at both *Opera House* and *Palace*. Indeed latterly Cochran moved his shows to the *Opera House*.

I saw strenuous rehearsal nights — Cochran and Coward on revue, Coward producing *Bitter Sweet,* Tom Arnold producing, Julian Wylie producing pantomime. Long anxious nights of hard work from which it was possible to emerge to dim early morning light.

There was a custom at the *Palace* which I hope still persists. Towards midnight there would be a break in rehearsal and there would be served delicious slices of specially made pork pies — Palace pie we called it.

The *Theatre Royal* and the *Princes* might have their pantomimes but otherwise they were homes of "straight" drama. During the heyday of the Aldwych farces touring versions were sent out and came to the *Princes*.

Humour at the *Tivoli* was pretty broad but the theatre had one feature which drew the crowd. There was a stalls bar which could be entered from the street where a barrel of Worthington stood on stillage on the bar. You were able to observe that your beer was drawn straight from the wood — and it *was* beer.

Opposite the *Theatre Royal* was the old *Cafe Royal.* There was a narrow bar with a background of giant vats from which wines were drawn — chiefly sherry — and one might find a connoisseur thoughtfully savouring the medium dry or the cream.

There had been a theatre lower down Peter Street, the *Comedy,* which I did not get to know as a theatre. I only found it when it became a cinema, the *Futurist!*

Manchester was for many years a great theatrical producing centre. It was regarded as a good place for a trial run before a London opening. And it produced components for shows. There were theatrical costumiers in a big way and up in Rusholme Tiller was training his dancing troupes. I spent just one afternoon watching him at work. He demanded absolute precision, a school of thought which is pretty general today, though at that time the Tiller Girls were in a class to themselves.

The building in Rusholme which housed the Tiller School was the old "Rusholme Office", in other words a big depot of the Manchester Carriage Company and of the horse trams. I knew every corner of it because it became first the *Rusholme Theatre* with a small but quite excellent stock company and then the *Manchester Repertory Theatre,* a limited company run by people anxious to keep the 'rep' movement alive.

I became involved because by this time I was writing about theatres for an evening newspaper and fell for the job of chairman of the Manchester Repertory Club which met on Sunday evenings using the stage and the auditorium. Actors, producers, writers, all came to talk to us and we had very exciting discussions.

The Second World War killed the Club.

It was just before the war that three people had an idea which they — quite independently of each other — communicated to the Manchester Director of Education, Lester Smith. The three were Gordon Bell, a repertory actor, W. L. Marsland, headmaster of a Manchester secondary school and myself. Each of us suggested the formation of a children's theatre organisation.

It was a time of cinema progress. There were cheap children's matinées everywhere indoctrinating the young in "the movie habit". One point on

Piccadilly, Manchester seen from the *Queen's Hotel* in the 1890s. Horse trams and cabs and the old Royal Infirmary on the left. The Queen Victoria memorial had not been erected.

Market Place and the Old Shambles before the Second World War. On the left the old *Wellington Inn*, the only building to survive the blitz.

which all three of us agreed was that the live theatre should have an equal chance or that children should have an equal chance of seeing live theatre.

Lester Smith brought us together and the outcome was the Adventure Theatre Guild which somehow survived the war and afterwards among other activities put on an annual drama festival for schools. I had a spell of years as chairman of the Guild.

There was another between the wars venture for theatre-goers with which I was never closely connected but which had inspiration from a good friend of mine, F. E. (Teddy) Doran. The venture was the Manchester Playgoers Club which entertained great ones of the stage and which organised parties to visit big London shows.

I was never a member of the Playgoers but they were kind enough to invite me to some of their very impressive functions. I remember in particular a supper party at the *Midland Hotel* at which Dame Sybil Thorndike was the guest of honour. I think she has always been fond of Manchester since she lived and worked here in repertory.

That evening in response to a very warm welcome she recited Shakespeare's address to audiences and I have never heard anything so appropriate and so well done.

Teddy Doran was a great figure in Manchester. Wherever there was artistic endeavour you were apt to find him. Of course he was a great propelling force at Rusholme. It was a privilege to know him.

I have mentioned my own efforts at playwriting. My first arose from an idea I put forward to Sir William Haley, then Managing Editing the *Manchester Evening News*.

Eric Wigham, now a veteran member of *The Times* staff, was then writing film news for the *Evening News*. Manchester was planning a celebration of the centenary of its incorporation.

"Why don't we present the city with a script for a centenary film?" I asked.

The idea was accepted and John Grierson, the great pioneer of British documentary film production, was engaged to collaborate so that my film technique would be acceptable to a producer. I did some weeks of research and produced a series of episodes with the title: *They Built a City*. As I produced instalments I took them to Soho Square to Grierson's office and he vetted the manuscript. On one occasion we did our deliberations at Harrietsham where he had a strawberry farm.

The script was run as a series of instalments in the *Manchester Evening News* and the illustrations were photographs of costumed tableaux of episodes posed by my colleagues on the newspaper staff. It was great fun but the film was never produced.

But Armitage Owen, the manager of the *Manchester Repertory Theatre* who wrote Lancashire character plays asked me to join with him in turning the script into a stage show. This was done and ran so well that the theatre was able to run longer into its summer recess than ever before in its history. There were enough royalties to give me a holiday in a rented seaside bungalow.

The other venture was an equally episodic show which I wrote in Prestwich at the time of the Festival of Britain and which was staged and produced excellently by local talent. It was called *Portrait of a Year*.

CHAPTER SIX

A Cedar Box

WHILE I was writing the preceding chapter, I opened a cedar box containing letters which over the years I had felt were worthy of preservation. Some were letters of commendation from editors — Sir William Haley for example — and you never know, you may need to produce evidence of your fitness for another job!

Among them was a handful of letters from Charles Blake Cochran and as I looked at them a flood of memories of great and glamorous occasions came to me. I was making passing mention of his interest in Manchester but I realised at once that I must write another chapter about him and about the period of great showmanship in which he was the leader and uncrowned monarch.

I suppose it is not unusual to be attracted by men who have a natural gift of showmanship — men who often take big chances in their efforts to entertain or to create. It must be obvious that the essence of showmanship is a spirit of daring; a readiness to take risks.

Every show of whatever kind is a risk. A theatrical production or a film or a pageant is presented and its success or failure depends on the fickle chance of public approval.

Charles Blake Cochran to whom knighthood came long after he had, in my opinion, fully deserved it, had tremendous courage. Once he had decided on a show to be done only the best of everything that could go to make it was good enough for him.

Of course, at the base of the structure was the judgement of a genius on whether a play or a script had any chance of success.

C. B. Cochran thrilled me because he was such an outstanding genius among showman and because he had such high regard for Manchester as a city in which to try-out a production. He discerned that Manchester was sufficiently intelligent and sufficiently sophisticated to tell him whether a show was good enough for the West End of London.

The Cochran years and particularly the years of the Cochran — Coward partnership were years of great glamour in Manchester. The *Midland Hotel* had clouds of glory floating above it for days, perhaps weeks before the opening night.

47

The *Princes Theatre*, Manchester built in 1864 demolished to make way for the building of Peter House, a modern block which accommodates some of the BBC departments.

Market Street, Manchester about the year 1890. Note the hansom cab on the right and horse trams in the distance.

Oh yes, I know that other towns have had great theatrical occasions but I am sure no town ever had such a firm reputation as a 'sounding board' as Manchester.

I don't remember how or when I first met C. B. Cochran. I know I was on the *Daily Mail* editorial staff at the time. We met and for some reason best known to him he decided that I was a newspaper man who would not try any tricks. As a clever showman, he had an unerring sense of how to make skilful use of publicity. He knew when and how much to release of the news of shows he was producing. He and his doings were always news. The bright boys of journalism were always trying to ferret out the secrets of the showman. Timing to him was the essence of success.

I suppose I should count it as one of my natural assets that I have always given an impression of being guileless and somewhat remote. Whether it was that tendency which made an impression I shall never know. What I have to record is that from our first meeting Cochran honoured me by keeping me fully informed of his intentions.

Very often he wrote in pencil in a great hurry. I didn't keep all his letters. It was safer to destroy some because he told me so much in confidence. That was the secret of the correspondence. He relied upon me not to tell Manchester more than he was ready to reveal.

At the top of the pile of letters in the cedar box is one which begins:—

"Dear George,

I see among my clippings several statements about plays for Manchester to be produced by me this autumn. It occurred to me that you might like to get the facts straight from the horse's mouth for publication or *NOT* as you think fit."

(The emphasis on the "*NOT*" is his.)

The letter ends "as this is written in a deckchair forgive the pencil and strange caligraphy".

This same letter continues, "After a long stretch of inactivity i.e. in the limelight — in my office I've been working like the devil —. (D. V. and Hitler V) to get busy.

"I have been reading plays and talking to authors ever since my return from U.S.A., last year. Many plays I have turned down have been produced by others without success.

It looks prosaic and utilitarian enough but it has history. The house was once the home in Manchester of the Grant brothers, friends of Charles Dickens and on whom he based his picture of the Cheeryble brothers. This photograph was taken in 1938.

"I have within the last week read a play of which I think most highly. It is historical. More I cannot tell you as no contract is signed yet but will be, I hope, very soon.

"Also oddly enough within this last week I've received a revised version of a play which I read and liked when I was in Hollywood but felt certain alterations were necessary. At the time the authors did not see eye to eye with me; now they do. My acquisition of this play depends upon whether the actress I want for the play will be free this year (she's in a success now) and if not whether the authors will agree to wait for her.

"Then I've got a book for a musical play which I'm really crazy about. It's in the hands of a composer now and this I hope to present in Manchester in November. There are sound business reasons why I cannot mention the authors and composers names YET.

"Lastly I am negotiating for a long lease of my favourite theatre and I look like getting it. If I do I shall open it with a Cochran revue which is already well-planned and will be seen first in Manchester, Liverpool or Newcastle. I promise it to be as exciting as anything I've ever sponsored in the revue field and despite many admonitions from many quarters that the public want *This* and the public want *That,* I shall follow my individual predilections and go all out for a revue thoroughly Cochran and utterly 1939 — 40.

"People want beauty, wit and melody more than ever and will welcome a change from lavatorial and cissy offerings.

"Why I can't say definitely Manchester will be the kick-off place is because the date must be dependent on the date of my acquisition of the London theatre. Newcastle is anxious to get a Cochran opening and I've been offered special inducements to go there but I should like to give Manchester the first look at the revue.

Bless you — as ever
Charles B. Cochran."

The date in the text of the letter is the only indication of date on it except the one word at the head, "Sunday".

The theatre he greatly favoured during a long period of successful revues was the *London Pavilion.*

Obviously the letter was written in a period of international uncertainties. It was typical of Cochran that he was not daunted. I do not attempt to identify the productions he wrote about. At that moment I became very quickly involved in the preparations for war. Others who were not so soon overtaken by war may be better able to remember.

THE

MANCHESTER

HERALD.

' The People have been too long the willing Dupes of
' defigning Men and interefted Meafures; they have been
' the Friends of the *Miniftry*, or the Friends of *Oppofition*, but
' they have never been their *own* Friends; while the fcat-
' tered few who have occafionally ftood forward in Behalf
' of the real Interefts of their Country and Mankind, have,
' firft or laft, been compelled to give Way before the cla-
' marous Accufations of Enthufiafm, Violence, and Inno-
' vation.'

Printed by M. FALKNER and Co.

There have been many attempts at newspaper publication in Manchester, some very successful. Here is the
title page of the Manchester Herald dated March 1792.

There is another letter — again in pencil and dated only "Sunday" which gives some detail of preparations for the production of *The Miracle*. It was necessary to arrange for removal of some of the seating at *The Lyceum* for the enormous set for this production.

"I think the production will be extremely beautiful" he says.

The letter then goes on to talk about the impending production of *Helen* which for the benefit of more recent generations I should explain was a lavish adaptation of Offenbach's *La Belle Helene*.

"Rehearsals are proceeding very well for Helen", he wrote, "we are held back a little by the work in the theatre as we are frightened to take our costumes out until the dirt of the builders is entirely out of the way."

This no doubt was reference to structural alterations at the *Opera House,* Manchester.

The letter continues: "Local interest is very high but Reinhardt producing Robey seems to intrigue the Manchester playgoer. Reinhardt cannot understand why."

Reinhardt had seen Robey doing his variety act as a German professor of music, which was very funny, at the *Holborn Empire.* Reinhardt thoroughly enjoyed a variety programme and was sure Robey was capable of playing Menelaus in *Helen.* Evelyn Laye was cast for the title role.

I have a much longer and much more detailed letter about this production. It is typed and is dated 26th November, 1931. I quote it here:—

"My production of 'Helen' in Manchester is about as big a theatrical event as anything which has happened anywhere in the last year or so. First of all, yours truly the boy producer is bringing Professor Reinhardt to your city. Unquestionably he holds a unique position in the world of the Theatre.

"I went to Berlin last year at the invitation of all the Berlin newspapers to assist at a series of banquets and festival performances which were given in honour of Reinhardt's twenty-five years work in the German theatre. Speeches were made by Ministers of the State, Heads of Universities, the French Ambassador, Hauptman the poet and other distinguished people.

"Seriously, Reinhardt is a very big man. The revival of 'La Belle Helene,' a classic opera-bouffe is an event in itself. Innumerable big names have been associated with it in the past. John L. Toole once played the part of Menelaus which Robey will play in Manchester. I saw Jeritza play the title role which falls to Evelyn Laye. Many distinguished comedians here and abroad have played Berry's part, Calchas. There is particular local interest in the engagement of Desiree Ellinger for Orestes.

"I don't want the public to get the idea that the costumes will be of the hard formal Greek classic type. Oliver Messel is aiming at the effect one gets from eighteenth century engravings of the heroes and heroines of ancient Greece and their gods and goddesses. The prevailing note will be baroque — just a little flamboyant.

"Korngold who has arranged Offenbach's music to suit A. P. Herbert's new book is a character in himself. He composed and orchestrated a ballet called 'The Snow Man' which was produced at the Vienna Opera House when he (Korngold) was only thirteen. Tilly Losch appeared as a child in it.

"Korngold will also come to Manchester. His more recent compositions have been popularised in this country by Elizabeth Schumann."

Market Street and its traffic in 1900. The streets were paved with granite setts. The tram on the left was going to Brooks Bar.

Much of the work of production of *Helen* was done in Manchester. Of course on these great occasions many people from London came up to Manchester to get a preview of that which "Cocky" as they nicknamed him, was bringing to the capital. Our hotels were crowded.

C. B. himself on this occasion rented the suburban home of a Manchester City Councillor for the long period he must spend with us. I was fortunate to be among those privileged to be entertained by the Cochrans. They had become very much "pro tem" Manchester residents. Of necessity they did much travelling and had developed a technique of carrying with them an atmosphere of homely hospitality.

In August of 1932 the year after the Manchester premiere of *Helen,* I received a picture postcard from the great man. It was posted in Dieppe and said:—

"Hope you're back from your holiday by the time I reach Manchester with my caravan. I was so tickled with the rehearsals under Noël's direction that I slipped away for a few days leave.

C. B."

It was a hint of tremendous things to come. The "caravan" was of course the entire company and all the etceteras of a big production — *Bitter Sweet.*

I suppose that though many people of my age and even younger may remember such gems of the Cochran-Coward collaboration as *Dance Little Lady* and *Mad About the Boy,* the show most often remembered *Bitter Sweet* and the theme most often played is *I'll See You Again.* What a Manchester opening that was! At the end people in the stalls at the *Palace Theatre* rose to give the show a standing ovation. People in rows behind climbed on to seats to see over the heads of those in front. It was a kind of hysteria of enthusiasm.

I have no correspondence about the show because I was very closely in touch throughout production. I sat very quietly at the back of the *Palace* while Noël Coward gave the production its final polish. The leading parts were taken by Georges Metaxa and Peggy Wood. There was an impressive atmosphere of confidence about the author-producer-composer as he stood in the orchestra pit at the *Palace* and about the players as they obeyed his instructions.

Max Beerbohm did a set of coloured cartoons of the principals in *Bitter Sweet.* A limited edition of prints of these cartoons was produced and Cochran gave me a folio containing the full set. I had them framed and hung in my house. When the house was bombed they were damaged — all except one — the cartoon portrait of Noël Coward. It hung precariously from an upstairs wall, an upstairs from which the floor had disappeared. Somehow, very gallantly a neighbour managed to get it down for me and I treasure it today.

A time came when things were not going wonderfully well for me. Cochran always managed to know what was happening to his friends. Came a knock at the door one day and a carrier delivered a case of a dozen bottles of Cochran sherry. With the case was a brief message:

"They can't keep a good man down."

I have a letter from C. B. addressed from the *Midland Hotel,* Manchester, and dated 28th September 1933. It says:

"I can't leave here without seeing you again. Could you look in for a drink and a sandwich about 6.30 tomorrow (Thursday)?"

Usually I saw him in crowded theatres or rehearsal rooms or an office. This was a rare occasion when he appeared to want to talk quietly in his hotel suite about plans and enthusiasms and the theatre. I met him for the last time in the *Adelphi Hotel,* Liverpool. By that time I was in the Civil Service, deeply involved in official publicity. I don't think he found this a very good idea.

Those letters have brought back many memories of much pleasure and much glamour and many hours among the stars.

They are back in the cedar wood box.

Do you remember when the City's Reference Library was housed in huts in a corner of Piccadilly gardens? This was it in 1929.

CHAPTER SEVEN

On the Calls

IT IS difficult to imagine that anyone could be able to see more of the seamy night life of Manchester than a reporter on the late calls. At least that was so in the days when I went the rounds on occasions. Not that Manchester has ever had a vast lurid night life.

Most recently I know the city has had a blossoming of night clubs. They were after my time and after all they are generally speaking pretty orderly places. That may be a disappointing and unpopular thing to say, but I'm sure it's true.

It was as the latest addition to the Manchester staff of a national morning paper that I was introduced to the late calls by one Stephen Williams, a wonderful bass singer later well enough known to B.B.C. radio audiences.

He was a picturesque figure wearing a walking stick as very much part of his appearance and crowned by a black felt hat, broad of brim. He led me into divisional police stations and police headquarters at the Town Hall. It was evident that he was known. We were amiably greeted.

We finished our round at Roby Street. Roby Street was the city's name for the central branch of the Manchester Royal Infirmary. It had I think a couple of wards and a largish reception area. It was in fact set up to deal with the emergencies arising in a city centre.

Today when ambulance speeds are more rapid and reliable and emergency techniques more advanced the accident and emergency cases go direct to the main hospitals.

I am harking back to days before it became a custom for police chiefs to call press conferences. Crime and accident reporting were very much a matter of luck, judgement – and persistence.

Maybe you detected a great deal of activity at a police station. In reply to your routine enquiry: "Anything doing?" one would get the equally routine reply: "No, sorry old man. Everything very quiet."

But stick around. Probably they won't order you out of the public part of the police station. They have the old fashioned candlestick type of telephone and when they talk everyone in the room can hear. A constable walks in and bangs a piece of evidence down on the desk. The best that can be said of

The River Irwell and Blackfriars Bridge. This picture is an important record because with two exceptions all the buildings seen here are now demolished. Picture taken in 1963.

eavesdropping is that its bad taste so we walk out into the street just in time to see a dishevelled looking customer brought in.

Some scared looking neighbours sidle up and stand around. "What happened?" you ask. "Smash and grab," says someone. "Jeweller's round the corner," says another.

So two and two begin to make four. The next move is a quick visit to the jewellers where detectives are spraying powder around in a search for finger prints.

That's a rough idea of how bits and pieces were picked up in my day "on the calls". With half a story one could approach authority and say, "what about giving me the official story?".

I had many police friends and I was given many stories of a kind which could not hamper the police in the job of preserving the peace. I was taken out in a police car to meet the police horses in their quarters and to talk to the men of the mounted section. I was invited to assist when a quantity of valuable cutlery was "recovered" before it had transpired that it was missing.

A very capable Inspector of my acquaintance was fond of embroidery as a hobby. To help a charity he persuaded people to pay a small fee to have their names embroidered on a table cloth which I believe was auctioned later. He gave me the story.

By the time I reached the Civil Service police attitudes had changed and there was a great deal of willingness to work with the press. But I don't remember that I ever had great cause to grumble.

There was a night when a man suspected of murder was traced to a house in a pleasant Manchester suburb. The police told us they were going out after him and I tracked them in an office car. The wanted man was in an upstairs front bedroom and was said to be armed.

Eventually a detective holding a highly polished cigarette case in his hand as though it was a revolver advanced to the foot of the staircase of the house and advised the man to come down. The wanted man hesitated, then fled to the bedroom. A shot was heard and he was found dead on the bed.

I wrote a story describing a dramatic dash by police and press in high powered cars. Well, no doubt we went quite fast enough for safety in busy city streets. But the police car available was a Jowett tourer and my car was an Austin 12 saloon which needed re-boring. For some time afterwards the wits of police and press circles lost no opportunity of asking me how my high-powered car travelling was going on.

I've got to talk about the hospitals. Not unnaturally the most productive source of news stories was Roby Street. If I was in town I never missed making a late call there. There was a night sister there on casualties who was a model of efficiency.

She was not very tall or muscular but she was tireless and she knew how to deal with any emergency. It was not unusual to go in there and find her dealing with a case of a broken head from some drunken brawl. She was prompt and merciless. All the hair must be shaved from around the head wound before the doctor stitched it.

She had a formidable cut-throat razor, officially issued to her. She knew that in those days I wore a very good leather belt. It was a lovely strip of leather left over from my military equipment.

"Just the man I want to see," she would say. "Where's the belt?"

I took off the belt and held one end while she stropped the razor on it. I believe she used that razor dry! She would advance into the accident cubicle and seconds later one would hear the cries of the wounded. The wound was exposed and cleansed and stitched. Often a policeman was standing by to march the sufferer off to the station.

Cases of alcoholic poisoning in various degrees were frequent. Fortunately it is likely to be more difficult to achieve such results today. People are better fed and liquor is of better quality and less potent.

The policing of the centre of Manchester in the period I am writing of — the "A" Division of that day — was administered from a headquarters in what was then Albert Street. It was a curious complex of buildings which housed the offices. It had started life as the headquarters of a gas company. When gas was first introduced as a luminant there was doubt as to the best method of distribution. There were experts who thought that main pipes should be run underground — under the streets. There were others who saw all kinds of drawbacks to this and who argued that gas should be sold in containers under pressure — as oxygen and other gases are distributed to this day.

The buildings in Albert Street were the headquarters of the company which offered coal gas in containers or tubes, whichever you like to call them. The street at the side of the buildings was Gas Street. There were offices fronting onto Albert Street, and behind was a big yard which was very useful for the stationing of police vehicles.

The whole complex was only demolished after the Second World War and today what is left of Albert Street has become Alberton Street.

Incidentally the first street lamp to be illuminated by gas was in Police Street which was the street leading to the Police headquarters of those far off days. You will find Police Street running parallel with Deansgate from St. Ann Street to King Street.

Since my nights on the late calls the work of the police has changed greatly; the devices at their disposal for dealing with it are vastly better than they used to be and co-operation with the press and other mass media of communication tends to be organised.

Do you know I remember the beginning of police wireless in Manchester! The installation was set up in an eighteenth century summer house on a hilltop in Heaton Park — at least that is where we were taken to hear about it.

To-day police radio oversteps the old boundaries of municipal and county systems. It must do so to keep ahead of fast moving law breakers. Even the constable walking on a country beat is in wireless contact. Up-to-date equipment to send and receive is housed in purpose built wireless stations.

A brave police horse faces one of those new fangled motor vehicles—an undated picture which tells its own story.

Police communications set up as it was and as it is.

Reproduced by kind permission of the Chief Constable, Manchester and Salford Police.

These buildings photographed in the 1780s stood at the corner of Cross Street and Market Street. They were demolished to make way for the Royal Exchange Building.

CHAPTER EIGHT

Clubland

A S IN many other towns and cities Manchester's clubland has tended to fade. Many masculine retreats have disappeared. Chiefly the trouble is that it is difficult to run an establishment which relies on midday patronage be it public house, eating house or club.

I have told of the activities of the Pack Drill Club. That was of a type of fraternity having no premises to maintain; no staff to pay; and meeting only in evenings.

Another organisation of somewhat similar character which I remember was known as John Shaw's Club. Members met periodically in those days at the *Queen's Hotel.* I was never privileged to attend one of the Club's gatherings though an account of its history was given to me for use in a newspaper article.

A very important part of its equipment was a fine old punch bowl, the contents of which were "discussed" at certain meetings. It was a most exclusive brotherhood. For all I know it may still be meeting somewhere in Manchester.

I look back however to a day when Manchester had a proliferation of clubs catering in many cases for groups of professional men. Do you remember the Brasenose Club in Mosley Street? It was a club with membership of doctors and consultants. Its premises are still there though recently they housed a branch of a building society. The Club lost ground and joined forces with the Reform Club in King Street.

The Union Club, as I knew it in Mosley Street, was in a lovely old building in plain Georgian stone architecture with a most ingenious front door. The hall porter saw you ascending the steps and by pulling a cord could open the door before you.

I think perhaps this old building had greater dignity than any other club premises in Manchester. The club owns some valuable paintings. In the old building one ascended to the top floor where one found members seated in semi-darkness around a billiards table on which light was concentrated. In this atmosphere after-lunch coffee was taken. I was never a member but often attended luncheon meetings there always with great satisfaction. The service and the nourishment were good.

Does this remind you of something you saw in Kensington Gardens, London? The Albert Memorial in Albert Square, Manchester.

The Clarendon Club, at the St. Peter's Square end of Mosley Street had a snug Victorian air. I have only very casual experience of its atmosphere but note it particularly because in the industrial depression of the '20s its members financed the adapting and furnishing as a club of an old warehouse building on the west side of Deansgate — that is behind the shops of Deansgate.

This was a club for men out of work and I hope was a great boon to many of them. It was given the title of Clarendon II. I remember being taken to the roof to admire the view over the city and looking down from that flat unfenced area I suddenly realised that my head for heights has its limitations.

I remember the Athenaeum when it was going strong. At that time there were eight art clubs in Manchester and they joined forces to organise a fancy dress ball in the Athenaeum Hall. I think it is fair to say that none of those attending were very wealthy but they had artistic genius and training and the costumes were marvels of ingenuity and wit. Supper was minced beef with boiled potatoes and we were furnished with a fork each with which to eat it. There were no tables and chairs were in very short supply so most of us took supper seated on the floor, our backs against the wall.

The Reform Club was much as it stands today, a rather florid Victorian building at the top of King Street — essentially the Liberal Club where Gladstone was said to have spoken and where a large medallion portrait of "Orator Hunt" (whose eloquence was drowned by the "Battle of Peterloo") decorated the entrance hall wall.

It is a curious fact that the Reform Club marched on when other clubs were foundering. When the Brasenose Club could no longer maintain its premises the members were accepted into the Reform Club. Indeed members from the Conservative Club at the corner of Cross Street and St. Ann's Street made their way to the King Street club when their own amenity closed.

The Conservative Club of which I speak still stands as quite a handsome building though now hacked around into shops and offices. Valiant efforts were made to save it in the years before the Second War. I remember Lord Derby — grandfather of the present Earl — calling the press to meet him there and he told us of the measures taken, to give the club new life. During the Second War this club became an American Red Cross Club for the troops.

In 1824 Mosley Street looked like this. The Portico Library on the left is still there but St Peter's Church in the distance has gone long since.

Manchester was ringed with captive balloons at that time, the idea being to frustrate raiding aircraft — a balloon barrage. In the midst of a very wet spell an American soldier looked out from the palatial windows of the former Conservative Club and said, "Why don't they cut the balloon cables and let the darned place sink?"

At the Milton Hall in Deansgate there was for many years a Congregational Club of which I had a visiting membership for some time though I am not a Congregationalist. It was a very chaste and pleasant place in which to meet pleasant people and eat a plain but well cooked luncheon.

But the club about which I know most and yet not nearly enough is the Manchester Press Club — the most itinerant and yet persistent club in the city. It is claimed that it is probably the oldest Press Club in the world though Birmingham and Barcelona may dispute that issue. It is more than a hundred years old — but my how it has travelled!

I first knew it when it was in a long departed building at the corner of Cateaton Street and Victoria Street. It was on the first floor and had a very small bar and a very efficient stewardess who superintended this bar and the catering. As far as I know the membership of the club has never been exclusive to journalists but there must be always a majority of journalist members. At the time of my first entry it had an artistic sprinkling of non-journalists.

Among these members was Charles Collier, cellist of the Hallé Orchestra who on special evenings entertained us with solos. Immediately before the Victoria Street premises the club had been in Pall Mall, I believe at the top of a very steep and long flight of stairs down which some members contrived to fall without hurting themselves too seriously.

After Victoria Street the club travelled around. Twice it was in cellar premises in the courts off Corporation Street. Once it was on the top floor of a building in Cannon Street. There was a long sojourn in spacious quarters in the basement of Blackfriars House — as friends and neighbours of the East Lancashire Territorial Association. These quarters had been planned by the Bleachers' Association as a suite for social activities which didn't mature — there was a war in the offing.

Though from the front of the building these quarters were in the basement, where Blackfriars Street descended the hill at the side they were near the ground level and at the back they looked out over a long drop to the level of the River Irwell.

The chemical constitution of the fluid in the river bed at this point has never been accurately defined. In fact it has been said that one could not fall *into* it and drown. More probably one would fall *onto* it and break bones.

A distinguished Lancashire journalist and novelist, James Lansdale Hodson, wrote a play for radio in the mid 1920s and included in it action in a boat. A small boat was borrowed and floated down to a point near Blackfriars House. It was reached from the window of an adjacent building. Characters in the play sat in the boat and produced the sounds of rowing by rhythmic splashing of the liquid of the river with pieces of board. The sound was very effective.

From Blackfriars House the club moved to a building in Albert Square — the old Memorial Hall, a Victorian religious monument and from that building it may move at any time. Recently members were kind enough to elect me as honorary member.

It is a curious fact that journalists do not take to midday drinking. Some of them use their Club for luncheon or a game of snooker or solo whist but the bar remains quiet. Before Giles achieved fame he did one of his funniest cartoons showing a journalist ordering a drink at a press club bar at lunch time. Everywhere around him and on both sides of the bar are shocked faces.

The Press Club treasures some cartoons in colour showing its celebrities of other days. Obviously Press Club custom comes usually in the evening in a city like Manchester which for long has been a centre for national morning newspaper production.

"The good old days"—not a motor vehicle in sight and look at the traffic snarl up! The Cross Street—Market Street crossing in May 1914.

One of these cartoons shows a late duty policeman lifting a street manhole cover to discover the source of noise and finding that he is looking down into the Press Club during one of its periods of cellar occupation.

I have not attempted a complete catalogue of all the clubs Manchester ever knew. It would demand a major research and would not suit itself to this kind of book. I have heard often for example of a very successful German club which flourished in Manchester before my time. I do know, however, that it left behind for many an ambrosial memory of really good German lager and hock.

There is just one other club of the activities of which I have happy memories — the Mummers' Club. In my day it met in an upper room at the *Abercrombie Hotel*. In its day the *Abercrombie* was a stage door pub to more than one Manchester theatre. The theatres disappeared but the *Abercrombie* soldiered on and found itself next door neighbour to a new "A" Division Police Headquarters.

It preserved a certain quaint bohemian quality which was very relaxing. One of its joys was that whichever half of the bar you were in — the "quality" or the "hoi polloi" you could see people in the other half.

The Mummers' Club in the heyday I remember was a haunt of people from the entertainment world. I have seen and heard some outstanding performances. One I remember particularly was a mind reading or second sight act which baffled me completely. There really was some mind reading.

The Club was very well run. It met on Sunday evenings — perforce because stage people work on the other evenings. There was a form of agenda very strictly adhered to and no excess in anything — even the humour. Always there was a collection for a theatrical charity fund and the money was taken up in a decorated frying pan. At a certain stage in the proceedings we sang "the Mummers' hymn". So far as I can remember it went like this:—

> "We Mummers Meet
> We Mummers Part
> With friendly hand
> And loving heart
> Content to help upon our way
> Each Mummer to a brighter day".

Yes, people of the theatre are sentimentalists — and they are genuinely warm hearted. I believe many a trouper down on his luck was helped along through the unpublicised generosity of the Mummers' Club.

CHAPTER NINE

Over the Bridges

IT WOULD be quite impossible for me to be nostalgic about Manchester as I remember it without recalling that across the River Irwell is another city with roots at least as deep and ancient as those of Manchester. No need to tell you that I'm thinking of Salford.

Though Mancunians rarely remember it and certainly never worry about it their ancient Hundred is the Hundred of Salford and this is the time honoured basis of local legal history.

To go from Manchester to Salford in addition to crossing a bridge in almost every case you go down hill. This is no reflection on Salford — just the result of the natural contours of the banks of the Irwell. The centre of the river is the boundary between the cities.

For hundreds of years there was only one bridge across between Manchester and Salford. It was the scene of a skirmish said to have been the beginning of the Civil War and appropriately enough the statue of Oliver Cromwell stood, until recently, near the site of the bridge.

The *Pictorial History of the County of Lancaster* published in 1844 says "the connection between Manchester and Salford almost amounts to identity; the same occupations are pursued in both; many who have places of business in one reside in the other, and the boundary between them is so narrow that it is crossed in a moment. This fealty did not always exist: the old bridge over the Irwell which was steep, narrow and inconvenient was continued from the fourteenth century until the September of 1837 when it was stopped by order of the authorities and a temporary wooden bridge erected preparatory to the taking down of the ancient structure and the building of a new bridge.

"This was chiefly owing to the exertions of the Manchester Improvement Committee; at their instigation the venerable bridge was indicted at the Quarter Sessions of Salford, October, 1836 for insufficiency of footway, roadway and waterway; not a single legal antiquarian appeared to plead for the antique pile; it was taken down and the new bridge was opened on the 20th of March, 1839, the anniversary of her Majesty's accession in whose honour the bridge received the name of Victoria".

It received much more. I remember when on the parapet at each side was a very large regal orb. Originally each of these was surmounted by a crown — the

A copy of a photograph taken in the 1890s and labelled as "Blackfriar's Street Manchester" which is worth reproducing here as a character and costume study of the period. There is no record of what they were all looking at.

Queenly crown — and at one time I believe there were gas lamps atop of the whole decoration. I believe the crowns were removed when Victoria died and I should say it was a great mistake because the bridge still bears the name and could quite appropriately bear her distinctive crown.

It has been noted many times in the past that Manchester is a commercial city — a city of offices and warehouses — and that the things which the outside world regards as symbolic of Manchester interests are not in the city at all. Probably the most quoted of these anomalies is that the docks which terminate the Manchester Ship Canal are chiefly in Salford. "If things go well they are the Manchester Ship Canal or the Port of Manchester. If things go badly they are Salford Docks".

The Old Trafford Cricket Ground is in the Borough of Stretford. The Manchester United football ground is in the same borough. Exchange Railway Station, now disused, is in Salford. And so it goes. True it was always pointed out that Manchester had the great northern University but even that balance has been upset because Salford now has its University too.

As you can see there's a pretty keen rivalry.

This has been largely due to the fact that Salford has been determined always to resist amalgamation.

Well, Exchange Station is closed now and Manchester City with its ground in Manchester is doing very well.

Though the lives of Manchester and Salford have long been closely inter-woven the two cities differ widely in character in many ways. Salford it seems to me always has closer affinity with Liverpool than with Manchester. Probably this is because Salford is a dockland city and a city with a large Irish Catholic population.

Salford became a city in the 1920s just after the great post-war Wembley exhibition. But it did not acquire a Lord Mayoralty. It has a Cathedral and a Bishop but they are Roman Catholic.

In my Grammar School days we had a developing sports ground at The Cliff, Higher Broughton, which is in Salford and from there we set out on cross country runs.

The many great mansions in Higher Broughton were still the homes of wealthy Manchester merchants and shippers. The Greek Orthodox Church was, and still is, in Broughton and the population was, and is, cosmopolitan. In those days the foreign residents were very wealthy people who readily supported artistic endeavour in Manchester. They thought of themselves as of Manchester.

One of the best known schools for girls in the north, the Broughton High School, inhabited a mansion which had changed its purpose. In the high garden wall of the High School was a letter box which still bore Victoria's Royal

The Flat Iron market in Chapel Street, Salford, in 1894. Note that small boy inspecting an umbrella on the right.

The old Blackfriars Bridge, the only bridge between Manchester and Salford in ancient times, as it was seen in 1825.

Monogram. It was a lovely survival which has now been corrected with hammer and chisel. Right on top of the Cliff was the Deanery. There I interviewed Hewlett Johnson who was then Dean of Manchester and a great figure in the city. When he preached at Manchester Cathedral it was something to see the congregation lining the pathway along which he would leave the building after the service. In those days he had not acquired the "Red" label.

We Grammar School boys used Salford also for the facility of a swimming bath. We went to the Blackfriars baths to practise life saving and under water swimming. There were times when the water looked very yellow and uninviting and smelled very strongly of chlorine.

I have always admired the Crescent, that arc of Georgian houses in Salford, built round a curve of the River Irwell. Close by was Peel Park with its museum. This museum — an adapted mansion is still functioning though surrounded by University and technical buildings. One hopes it will be kept, though there are plans I hear.

Old Salford has disappeared very rapidly. In great measure this is due to the fact that the city is hemmed in by other authorities on every side. If it was to house its population under decent modern conditions it must build upwards. This it has done. The process has meant the disappearance of vast areas of Victorian cottage property. However Walter Greenwood's Hankey Park and Cross Lane still harbour remnants of the past.

Lofty blocks of flats have grown even where it was said they could never build on low-lying banks of the Irwell. The flats are on "stilts" of concrete so that they are well above any danger of flooding.

As I have indicated Peel Park has been a victim of the educational development of Salford. In my young days it had wonderful gateways in a romantic oriental style. The railings themselves were rows of spears and then came the great gates. They were the nearest thing Salford will ever have to the approach to Delhi or the Taj Mahal. Indeed they were the product of that period when we were most proud of our Indian Empire.

The pleasant pathways where Salfordians could escape from city noises are gone to make way for a huge car park. Young Albert and Victoria still gaze at each other across the frontage of the building which still houses library, museum and art gallery. Long may they remain. Victoria and Albert once came there — in an open carriage from which they did not alight.

Platforms were built between which the Royal carriage drove so that the civic dignitaries could be at a reasonable level to pay their respects to Majesty.

Another view of the Flat Iron market as seen in 1894.

The 1851 Royal visit to Salford. The procession at Windsor Bridge Arch, Salford.

Illustrated London News

But it was made clear that it was just a matter of formal greeting on passing through and not a Royal Visit to the town.

It was clever to build a reconstruction of an old Salford street on the ground floor of the museum. I hope that somehow this venture can be preserved. I have not visited it for some years but as I remember it, it had a sweet shop, a clogger's, a smithy, a chemist, an old pub, a Victorian drawing room and an eighteenth century drawing room with Tudor undertones, cobbled streets, an ancient pillar box, an equally ancient brougham and, I think, a fire engine — not so extensive as York museum perhaps but equally authentic.

Whoever would think of finding bananas flourishing in Salford?

I hope it is still the custom as I remember it to have been for the reigning Mayor of Salford to hold a garden party in Buile Hill Park. This park and its hall are more survivals of the days before the internal combustion engine took the affluent further from the hearts of cities. Today the hall is another municipal museum and its greenhouses are a welcome gift to the city's parks department. Here I have seen bananas ripening — though I was never invited to sample them.

Dockland is a world on its own — surprisingly big ships look down on missions to seamen, small houses, pubs where you may eat or drink. Great articulated lorries emerge from the harbour complex with merchandise in exchange for the wealth of Lancashire goods which goes abroad.

The Port of Manchester extends throughout the length of the canal.

I have sailed on a Dutch cargo vessel from Salford docks to Amsterdam. It was a most interesting journey. The skipper spoke perfect English — no accent at all — and was a most courteous host. We sailed down the Ship Canal and when the tide permitted we were locked out into the Mersey whence we sailed right around the south of England, up the North Sea and the North Sea Canal to Amsterdam. The boat had been built for eastern trade and, therefore, was well ventilated. The Dutch cooking was excellent.

October 1851 and Queen Victoria with Prince Albert enters Peel Park, Salford. They were on their way south from Scotland and used the railway!

My other great canal adventure was aboard a destroyer. There was to be a Naval visit to Manchester and the flotilla was sailing from Arran to Manchester.

I boarded one of the destroyers from Arran and found that the vessel to which I was assigned had to finish a training shoot on the journey down the Irish Sea. There was much consternation because one of our torpedoes went off course. It had been fired with a dummy head. It was recovered and dismantled so that a court of inquiry could examine it.

In the Ship Canal the canal pilot who came aboard introduced me to a curious phenomenon. A vessel in any of the locks is powerfully attracted towards one side or other of the lock — a kind of capillary attraction. The pilot's anxiety is to keep the vessel from hitting the side. Destroyers being lightly built were strongly subject to this strange magnetism.

The Ship Canal opened in a vintage year — the year I was born.

There is a very special memory which I must put on record in this chapter because it is a record of a Salford institution which has vanished without leaving a trace. Did you ever visit the Flat Iron Market? It was a strange institution. At the foot of Blackfriars Street not very far into the City of Salford one came on this busy scene. It was always a matter of wonderment to me that so much activity could be crowded into so small a space. On two scraps of land near Sacred Trinity Church, stalls were set up and junk of all kinds was offered for sale.

"Junk" is the only word I can think of to describe the collection of strange objects — largely hardware — offered to the public. There *were* flat irons but I never discovered whether the market had its name from the merchandise or from the shape of the plot of land on which it stood.

There were old door locks, oil lamps, fire-irons, bunches of keys, gramophones, pieces of harness, second-hand tools of various kinds — sometimes second-hand shoes and hats. It was an extraordinary medley in which you might find a spare part long out of production to help you repair a lawn mower, a bicycle, a sewing machine, or even perhaps a motor car.

The Flat Iron had had its great days. I have been told that long ago there was a tiny fit-up theatre offering melodrama on one of the plots of land. Modern traffic found the market a nuisance. It never could have survived. The Church which was its neighbour is a pleasant refuge from its environment though nowadays it has shrubs and other greenery beside it.

Soon after the Flat Iron Market disappeared the adjacent branch police station went out of business. A busy corner of Salford became respectable!

Salford is reached by crossing bridges. Whichever way you go in it seems that there are bridges — some of them railway bridges. But the name of the city suggests that there were no bridges when the place was born. I'm told that Salford is really "Shallowford" gone a little peculiar.

Anyway I don't see how anyone could write about Manchester without mentioning Salford.

In 1894 Queen Victoria came to Manchester to open the Ship Canal. Here is Market Street decorated for the occasion and with local volunteers on guard awaiting the Royal progress.

CHAPTER TEN

Welsh Hymns and Brass Bands

I BET there are not many reporters who have worked against the clock to hit a morning paper deadline with strains of a hymn sung in Welsh floating in at the window! I have.

When I joined the *Daily Mail*, Deansgate, Manchester, staff after the 1926 General Strike there was a small but quite elegant Welsh Wesleyan Chapel almost surrounded by *Daily Mail* building.

When the site was acquired for the building of the newspaper office for some reason that small building was not bought. Later a high price was paid for it to make possible the erection of big new offices. But in those days I remember services were still held in the Chapel and on Sunday evenings as we bashed out copy for Monday morning's paper we heard the music of the service. No one minded. It was an accompaniment *not* an interruption.

By the way I have heard some very good people say that they would never buy Sunday papers because they make people work on the Sabbath. I wonder when they think the work of production goes on for a Monday morning paper?

I'm looking back to a time when it seemed there was much religious worship and activity in the centre of Manchester. I'm not setting out to catalogue in full the forms of worship which were observed. My purpose as in the rest of this book is to let memory wander among the pictures it has treasured. One which comes back to me very vividly is of a Saturday evening at the Albert Hall. This Hall as you must know is one of the depots of the Manchester City Mission — a Methodist activity. Its future is in the balance.

Saturday evening you paid sixpence for admission and found yourself a member of a packed audience — not you will observe of a "congregation".

Perhaps there was a prayer and the singing of a hymn but the main business of the evening was a grand all-embracing entertainment. There was often a brass band — or a band of some kind. The show I remember best had a high quality Salvation Army band. I am a northerner and love brass bands. As a teenager I used Sunday afternoons to walk in a park and listen to a brass band.

There was one item which was never missing from a park programme. It was — you've guessed! — *Morning, Noon and Night* by Suppé.

"The Hidden Gem"—the pulpit of St Mary's Roman Catholic Church, Mulberry Street, Manchester.

One of the Whit Week processions in Manchester in 1938. Those overhead tram wires were a menace when you were carrying a banner, particularly if it was a breezy day.

Let me get back to the Albert Hall and the Salvation Army band. A brass band in the open must accept the climatic conditions as they come. In a hall there is no high wind to blow the sound away. Nor is there noise of passing traffic. When I was a youngster I worried a little about brass bands indoors. It seemed to me credible that some beautiful sweet note might shatter the chandeliers or bring the ceiling down. You see I'd heard the story of the vocalist or violinist who hit a note which did just those things.

That Salvation Army Band brought the house down in a more pleasant sense. There were two very good vocalists, a baritone and a soprano.

Finally a screen descended from the roof and a feature film was shown — not a religious film, a genuine down to earth feature.

And I believe that at the interval if you could squeeze your way out from your seat there was a tea bar where for a penny you could buy a cup of tea. What a joy those shows gave to a lot of people with not much money and not much fun in their lives! Many of them I believe returned morning or evening on Sunday to take part in the religious service.

I've mentioned the Dean's services at the Cathedral in another chapter. At this same period there was at All Saints Church in Oxford Road the Rev. Etienne Watts. However he may have been criticised — and he was criticised — he was a man of infinite compassion. Just behind his Church were the old Public Assistance Offices — the last unhappy resort of the flat broke.

This circumstance meant that on the broad footpath in front of the church there assembled many very desolate, hungry people. It was a period of industrial stagnation in many fields. The flotsam and jetsam drifted to All Saints. Of course there were old sea lawyers among them — intelligent types who took the trouble to read up the rules and for a Woodbine or a copper would advise on how to get maximum help from 'P.A.' or 'The Labour'.

Mr. Watts preached some fiery sermons on conditions as he saw them around him.

It was the heyday of the wayside pulpit. Cross Street Unitarian Chapel had very much set the pace. The wayside posters put up at All Saints were calculated to shock. Today they might well have seemed easily acceptable. We take a great deal of shocking. Probably we are punch drunk. But in that day and age there was much anxiety about Bolshevism. Russia had turned Bolshevik!

After all Lenin's great idol was Karl Marx who had worked on his economic theories in this very city!

It was so very disturbing to people who only asked the Church for reassurance in their expectation of eternity. Here was a vicar who criticised a social system which let men rot for want of a job. No wonder there was criticism of the vicar!

St Peter's Church. The City War Memorial Cenotaph now stands where the church once stood. An ornamental cross commemorates the church and for the rest there is a small garden and a square of stone seats much used on fine summer days.

Came the Second War and tragedy struck All Saints. The Church was destroyed by enemy action. The tower contained a great deal of manuscript church music of great value and I'm afraid a great deal of it was destroyed.

If I think back to the days of my boyhood I can recall the period when Father Bernard Vaughan was preaching at the Holy Name Roman Catholic Church beyond All Saints in that same Oxford Road. I think he created as great a stir as the Rev. Etienne Watts though he only frightened the wayward few. He preached against the sinfulness which he saw in the main street outside his Church. He called that stretch of Oxford Road "the devil's mile". He made things difficult for the street walkers, the ladies of easy virtue, and their clients.

If you wanted stimulation you went along to the Oxford Road Churches. It was not surprising that people of various denominations filled the seating at both the Holy Name and All Saints.

Of course I could write at length about Manchester Cathedral. I suppose any Old Boy of the Grammar School of my period could. It was the school Church. We went there to remember our founders. For years I was a member of the Executive of the Manchester branch of the Council of Christians and Jews. It is a body on which are representatives of most denominations — including Jewish denominations. Each year we organised a Brotherhood week during which Church and Synagogues were open to the public in general. I hope the activity persists. Guides volunteer to show people round the place of worship about which they have knowledge.

During one of these weeks I joined a party going round Manchester Cathedral. I was interested to find a Jewish friend of mine — a solicitor — leading a party including Jews and non-Jews and talking about the features of the building with great affection. I expressed surprise that he should be doing this. "Why not?" he asked. "I went to the Grammar School and this was our Church."

Equally I have spent a great deal of time attending services in Synagogues — the Holy Law on the Manchester Prestwich boundary which is 'orthodox' — the Jackson's Row Synagogue in the centre of the city which is 'reform'. They have their differences of approach but their faith is embodied in the Books of Moses which Christians may find in their Bible but which they read most rarely.

My willingness to be interested in any form of monotheism has brought upon me before now an accusation of "indifferentism". I don't know whether that's a *very* bad thing. It means that you don't mind how people worship as long as they worship.

Manchester's Society of Friends has a history of steadfast faith. Their building is in Mount Street and its distinction is that it is the only building existing which was standing in the neighbourhood of and at the time of the Peterloo happening. I take it you've heard about that. It is referred to variously as a massacre, an affray, a disturbance, even as a riot.

The Friends' Meeting House looked out on the turmoil but preserves its palladian equanimity. At that time the area before the Meeting House was St. Peter's Fields and I suppose the Church of St. Peter was still there. The affair interests me because it proves that even a journalist can allow himself to be influenced by the treatment he receives!

When mounted troops were turned loose on a crowd of millworkers the *Times* representative found himself in the midst of the 'rough house'. He extricated himself with difficulty and set off for London where he wrote a stinging report of the way the Manchester Magistrates had dealt with a demonstration. It may be very unfair of me but I've wondered always what he was most indignant about — the treatment he'd received or what he had seen!

That was 'way before my time but it may encourage you to take a look at the Friends' Meeting House. Its inside has received some modernisation, there was considerable unused space, but in essentials it is still itself.

Now let us go along to St. Ann's Church, essentially the Church of the city centre of the business quarter. I have spent many hours in there at Lenten services and Christmas Carol services particularly. Take a look at the pulpit. It is very tall and very beautiful and to avoid cutting it down and impairing its beauty they have made it stand in a shallow well. John Wesley once preached from it.

When Canon Paton Williams was the incumbent, this church was visited by the Duke of Kent. I was very proud to find myself on a photograph of the visit hanging in the vestry.

Leave St. Ann's and come through St. Ann's Passage into King Street, cross King Street and you will find the continuation of the passage way between shops opposite — a very ancient right of way.

Continue through St. James' Square and find the continuing passage between shops again on the far side of John Dalton Street. It leads you to a passage to Mulberry Street, a very secluded backwater, and here is "The Hidden Gem", a small Roman Catholic Church — a quiet and lovely retreat from the bustle of the city. Many times when it has been my duty to look after the welfare of overseas visitors who wished to go to Mass I have shown them "The Hidden Gem". Once a member of my staff was married there. The outside is austere — lofty brickwork and too hemmed in for one to appreciate it. If you are round that way go in and look at the carving of the altar.

The Roman Catholic Church of the Holy Name in Oxford Road where Cardinal Vaughan, as Father Bernard Vaughan, preached great sermons.

CHAPTER ELEVEN

Reaching the Hearts of Men

WELL, of course you reach a man's heart through his stomach -- or so they do say. Certainly the world is always a much better place when I'm nourished than when I'm hungry. Even lions are better tempered after they've fed.

Manchester's catering habits have changed a lot in my years of observation — but then they are always changing. Chiefly I have seen the change from the days of universal joint and two "veg" to days of instant grill — and chips. Always there are chips.

Even so it isn't easy today to find a place where you can admire a selection of steaks and chops on the chef's table and choose the piece you will have grilled. I can remember a few such places. Some may still function in slightly changed form. There were specialities that were worth knowing about.

There is a very elegant efficient and popular *Sam's* restaurant in Manchester today. I remember its ancestor, a restaurant in a basement entered from Market Street where they had a dish which I enjoyed and which could be expected to appeal to most men. Its feature was simplicity — a large steak and kidney pudding with a large floury potato baked in its jacket. A friend of mind considered that their soups also were special.

About the same time *Thomas's Chop House* in Cross Street offered another rarity of which I was very fond. One could have a bowl of very good soup followed by a dish of very large and succulent mussels.

These of course were not the dishes for the ladies. If one was entertaining there was *Parker's* in St. Ann's Square, a lovely Victorian restaurant with deep and closely buttoned upholstery.

Afternoon tea could be in the best of social traditions with China tea, of course, if you insisted. Not far away in St. Mary's Gate, *Parker's* came down to the level of the man in the street with a licensed bar specialising in bottled *Guinness*. For a shilling you could feast on soup with hot roll and a *Guinness*. Upstairs was a robust restaurant where the joints with "veg" were served in good style.

Many people mourned the passing of the *State Cafe*, a Joseph Lyons institution in Piccadilly which offered service and catering in a superior manner. The management would rise to any occasion. For a birthday party at short notice

In 1866 St Ann's Square was nice and tidy like this. Later a cabman's shelter with kitchen and cook stood in the centre. Now there is a taxi rank and a South African war memorial.

the chef would prepare one of those puddings — hot outside and ice cream within — with the name of the guest of honour imprinted on it — and birthday wishes. This dish was brought in to musical accompaniment provided by a resident orchestra.

It was perhaps a working lad's *Ritz*, but then we be simple country folk living north of Watford and dressing in woad. The *State* went to provide space for some new shops.

For less lavish occasions I found refuge very often in the *Waldorf Cafés*. There were several of them under that name. For a light meal on leaving the office to go on to an evening engagement I could have a small grilled steak with chips, brown bread and butter with a small jar of jam and a pot of tea for one shilling and ninepence.

The great places for celebrating an occasion were of course the big hotels. I can just remember the *Mosley* and the old *Albion* in Piccadilly though I never darkened their doors. The ones I knew were the *Queen's*, the *Grand,* and "that new palace the *Midland*".

Opened at the beginning of the century the *Midland* had then as now a French restaurant but below ground was also a German restaurant with excellent Teutonic food and drink. I wonder how many people remember that the *Midland* had a theatre?

What is now the main ground floor ballroom was the auditorium and the Alexandra suite was the foyer. I remember seeing the Follies there and who now remembers Pelissier and the Follies?

There were Smallman's *VEM* restaurants in those days (vegetables, eggs and milk) and of course here the salads were special. In the Victoria Building which housed the *Victoria Hotel* and many interesting old businesses was *Hailwood's Dairy* which pleased one with a glass of buttermilk now and then. In that same building was a shop with an inscription "Smithy Door" in each corner of its plate glass window. There is a curious title which stipulates that the Smithy Door must always be signposted at this spot. What happens about it now that the area is being massively developed?

Sainsbury's have been feeding Manchester business men for a very long time. I remember my father speaking of having a snack in *Sainsbury's* and that was a long time ago.

And there was the *Bodega* which became the *Stock Exchange Restaurant*. And there was a small but very choice restaurant in Pool Fold off Cross Street. In the underground regions of the Royal Exchange was the *Manchester Limited*

Levers' Hall, town house of the Levers of Alkrington, once stood where the *White Bear Hotel* stood later. Then the *State Cafe* was built on the site. The *Mosley Hotel* made way for a cinema which is now Littlewood's store. There are shops now on the *State Cafe* site.

Beginning of Oldham Street—Piccadilly end—in 1894 showing on right the *Albion Hotel* which disappeared to make way for a Woolworth's store.

with cubicles where business men from the Exchange floor above could foregather for a coffee or a meal. We held several Manchester Press Balls down there.

I've mentioned already the *Squirrel* restaurant started by Arno Rolls after the First War.

In Deansgate for many many years was a pastry cook's shop with the names Godbehere and Scott over the window. The lovely name of Godbehere probably of Puritan origin greatly pleased me. If you went upstairs you found a restaurant where you could have a hot pork pie fresh from the bakehouse oven — very rich — very lovely.

Manchester has always had a goodly share of delicatessen shops. One of the best known of these has always been *Titanics* so called because the founder of the firm was a survivor from that great maritime disaster.

There were Jewish establishments in Cheetham Hill Road where I could buy delicious pickled meat — melted in one's mouth it did. In Stretford Road was the *Scotch Shop* and here one bought Scottish loaves — crust on top only — and Scottish soda scones.

I could go on at great length about Manchester as a place to eat — I haven't talked about the theatre restaurants — the *Café Royal*, the *Princes* and the *Palace* as I remember them. I haven't talked about the excellence of *Frascati's* in Oxford Road. There isn't time or space to do justice to everyone.

I must mention however, the somewhat unique catering of the Yates firm. The founder established wine lodges where good and reasonably priced wines can be bought. Also he established restaurants for good eating and baking and butchering establishments. He believed that it is wrong to slaughter frightened beasts in an abattoir. They should be taken unaware in the fields and humanely killed. He set up a farm at Bosley in Cheshire and advertised Bosley Beef.

In Oldham Street he opened a *Coffee Tavern* where food and hot drinks were offered at very reasonable prices. I believe these places are still known as *Teetotal Taverns*. Mr. Yates was a great benefactor in his own special and original way.

A sixteenth century, house, home of the Sydall family, in Smithy Door, a thoroughfare on the site cleared in 1875 to build the *Victoria Hotel*. The house, at time of demolition was an inn, the *Vintners' Arms*, colloquially known as Deakin's Entire. A portion of house occupied as provision merchant's business. To the right is Deansgate and behind St Mary's Gate.

In the days when Cotton was King the Royal Exchange — always a textile market place — grew and grew until it could boast that it had the biggest exchange floor in Europe certainly and probably in the world. Tuesday was the big market day and mill owners, yarn agents, textile machinery agents and representatives of all the auxiliary trades and crafts flocked in from the whole of East Lancashire, North Cheshire and the Peak District to do business.

From about ten o'clock in the morning they were coming out to take coffee and often to talk business over a table. Presently many of them were invading the licensed houses particularly in the Shambles and Old Market Place. Then restaurants and snack bars became crowded. Always there was emphasis on regular custom. There were seats or tables reserved every Tuesday and probably Friday — the other Market Day — for regular customers. Woe betide the stranger who walked in and sat down in a time honoured reserved place.

Much business was done in the streets or on the steps of the Royal Exchange. Some firms never took up membership of the Exchange. It *was* very expensive even for those far off prosperous days. Their representatives stood on the steps of the Exchange waiting to catch customers as they went in or came out.

It was a common sight to see spinners testing the staple of a raw cotton sample by drawing it out on the sleeve of their jacket while sitting at a café table or even standing on the pavement of St. Ann's Square.

It was always a short and intensive business day. I was told that "High Change" came at three o'clock in the afternoon and thereafter the Exchange floor rapidly emptied. This meant that there were two styles of eating — very hurried or very protracted. Coffee, aperitif and luncheon could use most of the business day.

Truth is that many men did not need to travel to Manchester every week. I have heard of one mill owner at Wigan who visited the Exchange once a year to buy raw cotton and once a year to sell his grey cloth.

But many many others would travel in every week to keep in touch with business colleagues and of course to watch the market.

I have wandered off at such length to talk about the Cotton Trade because it was to so large an extent a ruling factor in the minds of caterers.

Market day business alone would not keep open the doors of a restaurant. But it did bring to town some thousands of robust eaters who believed in combining business with gastronomic satisfaction.

The clerks and porters and people of lowly station generally had a friend in *The Lockhart* establishments. The bread and butter was not cut so thin, the tea

The *Fatted Calf Hotel* which was reached from Market Street by way of a narrow alley. There are those who claim that it was here the National Union of Journalists was founded. There was a quaint reading room with brass paper racks—gone! All gone!

and coffee came in cups — not in pots, the joints and two veg and stews and made dishes were plain and wholesome and the prices would not be believed today.

In one chapter of my life I got up very early in the morning and went into a newspaper office to put an early edition "to bed" for 8.00 a.m. That job done I went out to breakfast. The one place I could rely on to be open and ready to cook for me a hearty English breakfast of bacon and egg with a pot of tea and lashings of bread was a *Lockhart's*.

A happy memory and a happy note on which to close this chapter.

In 1894 experts appraise the value of a horse. A scene at the corner of High Street and Thomas Street.

CHAPTER TWELVE

Twinkle Twinkle Machine

"LADIES and Gentlemen, this is not the twinkle twinkle machine. This is actuality in miniature."

The speaker was a glamorous type with what he believed to be an American accent. He wore a white double-breasted suit and white felt hat and addressed the public through a megaphone. He was the 'barker' on the front of a show on Blackpool, South Shore, and he was publicising a show called *The Battle of the Monitor and Merrimac*.

It was said to be a reproduction of the first maritime encounter in which an Ironclad took part and was straight from some American amusement park.

The point the gentleman was making was that this was not a cinema show. It was a reproduction using clever lighting and electrically controlled models. There was no wireless remote control about it. We hadn't gone so far. But there was development of the cinematograph and it was a medium in which there was plenty of room for improvement.

My first exposure to the cinema was in a fairground marquee. There was a magnificent organ blaring on the front and from time to time a 'barker' dressed as he imagined a cowboy would dress stepped out onto a platform and invited us to come in to see the last of the Sioux or Cherokees or Mohicans. In other words here was the first of the 'westerns' — horses and waggons and guns and tomahawks.

I paid twopence because I was young and small and I sat with others on a very narrow straight wooden bench. We sat there a long time because they wouldn't waste electricity running the film until they had a good audience. When we did see the film it lasted only about a quarter of an hour. Of course it was black and white and it was very jumpy.

I suppose the conditions in which those films were shown would horrify police, fire authorities and insurers today. As I have said the structure in which we sat was really no better than a marquee with plenty of gaily painted woodwork about it. The films were celluloid with no fireproofing treatment and the projector was at best in a bit of a wooden box cabin or at worst set up on a platform at the back of the hall. The noise of the projector was terrific — when the organ piped down for a minute to let you hear it.

It seemed incredible that within a year or two the film show had so advanced and so taken hold that there were permanent buildings — movie palaces — where

Heaton House as it was seen in 1795. To-day we know it as Heaton Hall and it is the hub of Heaton Park. A modern tea room has been built onto the wing on the left. It was bought by the city from the Wilton estate.

films were the great attraction. Perhaps memory is deceiving me. Perhaps it took a little longer for the cinema to develop.

I have been told that the first regular use of it was at the old *Argyle Music Hall* at Birkenhead. The management were very enterprising and they saw possibilities in the use of film to fill a spot in a variety programme. They used a wet screen. It was lowered from the ceiling and water ran down its surface as a reflecting medium.

The idea spread fast enough. It filled a spot in the bill to run one of the early comics — even Chaplin films came in in this way. Usually it was at the end of the show when people were getting up from seats and pulling on overcoats.

It may be a shock to some people to know that the cinematograph killed a form of entertainment. This was the panorama show. These shows came to the fringe of Manchester under various titles — panoramas, dioramas, myrioramas. They were marvels of ingenuity. Largely effects produced by the use of the big old fashioned magic lantern. Often two of these projectors were used so that pictures melted into one another.

Oddly enough the same technique is revived today by county lecturers using modern colour transparencies. These old shows went further. There were mechanical slides with movement engineered by having double glass and levers. Also there was physical scenery and there was coloured lighting.

For the more moving portions of the programme — as for example slides illustrating *The Miner's Dream of Home* there would be a vocalist with piano accompaniment.

When the cinema developed it was a case of one twinkle twinkle machine giving place to another. The cinema was so much more flexible. The programme could be changed so much more easily. But in the early days none of us foresaw the cinema boom which was coming — that is none of us simple souls, the general public.

When it did come its producers played with its flexibility. Motor cars did amazing things railway trains became airborne and set out for the moon. The lack of sound was an early problem. Orchestras in the city cinemas and pianists in the suburbs did their best to provide appropriate noises. In the top cinemas there were other sound effects. I remember a film called *The Four Horsemen*. The reference was of course to the Apocalypse. It was a war film. There were synchronised noises culminating in the firing of a maroon which shot half the audience off their seats.

Firework displays were for many years a main attraction at Belle Vue Zoo, Manchester. They were always topical and were staged on an island in a small lake. This one was the 1908 feature and reproduced the siege and relief of Mafeking in the Boer War. No T.V. in those days!

Then came an attempt at talkies — disc recordings with a dial on the front of the gramophone which played them. There was a similar dial on the film and the operator had to regulate his film speed to keep the two running together. It was an exciting novelty but not a great success.

My first talkie was *Sonny Boy,* an Al Jolson film which wallowed in sentiment. The action was slow because the system of sound recording and reproduction demanded it. It is curious to realise that there are many young people around today who can only think of films as with sound and colour.

I haven't localised this chapter very much because what happened to the cinema in Manchester is very much what happened in every town and city in the country. At the same time it must be recorded that Manchester had had its studio and its producers. Formby films were produced here among others. The 'talkie' feature I remember most vividly was *Hell is a City* made and given its premiere in Manchester. It includes a fearsome fight on the parapet of what was thought to be a high building. We have gone higher since then.

After the First World War we had in Manchester a tremendous showman, one Louis Blattner, who managed a cinema which occupied what had been Miss Horniman's *Gaiety Theatre.* Showmanship was in Blattner's blood. His publicity for his cinema shows was outstanding. Usually the programme included an act or speciality of some kind as well as a feature film.

One week two very charming young society ladies, the Ruthven twins, appeared on the stage. Veterans of the theatre were engaged to give readings. It was all vastly entertaining. Mr. Blattner became interested in the possibilities of tape recording, then very much in its infancy. He left Manchester for the film studios of the south and died there very sadly. He was a vivid personality and though some of his ventures startled many people he was live and in many ways he was in advance of his times.

Radio was seen menacing the cinema at the time of his passing. What he might have done with the new medium we can only guess.

CHAPTER THIRTEEN

City at War

"KEEP this forever in the imagination of the thoughts of the heart of thy people." Thus says the inscription on the Cenotaph in St. Peter's Square, Manchester, the city's war memorial. I have watched and listened to many people who were puzzled by it.

Of course, it comes from the twenty-ninth chapter of the first book of Chronicles and is part of King David's prayer of thanksgiving when the great men of Israel made their contributions to the store of precious metals and other material for the building of the temple. It is one of those quotations from the Old Testament which will stand a lot of thinking about — obscure, and yet is it? It means just that much more than could be expressed by just saying "may we never forget".

A southerner visiting Manchester said to me, "Wars have dealt lightly with your city." Is it true? I think not. It is true that the scars of war are well hidden. The visitor may never know that they exist. In the Second World War, Manchester lost no opportunity of demolishing any building which could be said to have achieved a condition which made it a danger to human life and limb. The holes were filled by tidying up operations. The big open spaces were the result of post-war clearance.

Manchester has had a very full share of militancy and belligerence, but it does not dwell on these things. Perhaps it is too willing to cover the scars and forget. That may be a fact which makes the war memorial inscription very appropriate.

In the Platt Fields area there is a Red Brook, so called because it once flowed red with the blood of fallen warriors. The history books don't tell me when or in what battle the brook was a defensive line.

The Romans came — the Twentieth Legion from Chester. They must have liked the place. There is no record that they ever repatriated. Of course they were not Latins. They were Friesian mercenaries.

The Danes came and Manchester kicked them out eventually.

Somewhere about where Victoria Bridge stands today the Cromwellian wars started.

Lord Kitchener in Manchester in 1915. The "Pals" Battalions of the Manchester Regiment march past the saluting base in front of the Town Hall. The blue uniforms were Corporation Tramway stores which came in handy.

In the eighteenth century Bonnie Prince Charlie led his rebellious army into Manchester and paused awhile. He had his headquarters at the *Bull's Head Hotel* and his Highlanders must have used up quite a lot of billeting space in the small town of that day. There is still a Palace Street in which once stood a house where Charlie slept.

To the South African campaign Manchester made its contribution as is testified by the memorial in St. Ann's Square. Quite a good piece of dramatic sculpture this!

Came the great 1914-1918 war and Manchester was not bombed or bombarded. True it nearly had a Zeppelin to itself! The great skyship trundling noisily along at sixty miles an hour some three thousand feet up got to the neighbourhood of Bury, Bolton and Holcombe but never found Manchester.

But only one Regiment in the British army raised more battalions than the Manchester Regiment and that was a county Regiment, The Northumberland Fusiliers. Wherever there were British troops there were Manchester men either in their city Regiment or in other units.

So many went, so many died, the flower of a generation. I came back in one piece but then I never regarded myself as being in the class of those likely to achieve great things. In war anything may happen.

How can one convey to the youth of today a picture of the early scenes in that war — the scenes in home towns I mean? We breathed a heady atmosphere which brooked no doubts. We should win of course. We were a small country but we had the Navy and we had the Empire. I remember meeting a friend of mine who had a flair for drawing a word picture of an event or a period. He never took to writing professionally which was probably a great pity.

We lost ourselves in our imaginings of war as it would be waged. There would be aeroplanes flying ahead of armies to spy on the enemy. There would be guns of tremendous range, and when the navy went into action what thunder there would be! As quickly as possible we must get old enough to join the army. We both got old enough without too much delay. My friend lost a limb in the last hours of the war.

There was great civic recruiting of the Manchester Pals battalions. The idea was that you went along and joined with your friends. They were battalions of the Manchester Regiment eventually, but at the outset they were very much the city's effort. They were quartered in tents and later in huts in Heaton Park. The Corporation had a great store of blue serge uniforms for its tramway drivers and conductors and these uniforms were issued to the Pals. I must say they looked very smart. They were piped with red and had polished buttons.

The Pals recruited and trained in a period when mystery was rife. We were all over-conscious of the importance of security. The most popular barber and

Moult Street—one side of the Manchester Guardian building in March 1912—the hour High Change, with members of the Royal Exchange seen in the background spilling out into the streets to do business.

gents' hairdresser in the neighbourhood where I lived disappeared. It was true that he was a German. He had answered his country's call and no doubt served faithfully in the German armed forces.

Local report agreed that he must have been a spy! The whisperers agreed that his job must have been to get his customers to talk so that he could gather information of military importance. I wonder what happened to him. He was a very good barber. He could shave with celerity and lightness of touch which could not be beaten. I'm sure he was innocent of any dubious activity.

Poor Arno Rolls, I've mentioned him before, who practised as a good interior decorator and designer was interned. His health suffered, but he came back after the war and opened restaurants which introduced Mancunians to very good continental cooking. He held cookery classes for housewives with culinary ambitions.

Well, amid the crop of rumours was one oft repeated that the Pals would never go overseas. They would be retained for home defence.

I was planning with a friend of mine to join the forces "before it was too late". The war would be over if we were not careful and then how should we feel if we had not won our share in the victory? This may sound terribly naive now but in those days we really knew nothing of what modern war might involve.

It is an oft repeated truth that the army always prepares for the next war on the basis of conditions prevailing at the end of the last war. In this case the last remembered war was South Africa. The army had learned to wear khaki, to use open order drill and machine guns. They signalled with heliographs and flags and great big noisy Begbie lamps. Field telephones were a novelty.

The soldiers we saw were the local garrisons at places like Bury and Ashton-under-Lyne — oh yes, and of course the Territorials and the Officers Training Corps units.

My friend and I, we made up our minds and, after the manner of the time, we told no one what we intended to do. We went to the recruiting station in Dickenson Street, Manchester. The building which housed it is still there but the street has lost its identity in the fever of new development. It ran along the side of the Friends' Meeting House in Mount Street. That Meeting House has looked out on a great deal of history.

It is the only building surviving today which formed part of the fringe of the fields in which the "battle" of Peterloo took place.

It was an irony that this building which has been a citadel of conscientious objection to war should look out on so much belligerence and preparation for belligerence.

We went to the recruiting station and we were greeted by a very splendid recruiting sergeant. You don't see them around nowadays. Instead the armed services spend much money in advertising on television and in publications of various kinds. This recruiting sergeant had the red white and blue ribbons which were traditional attached to his khaki cap.

"And what can I do for you young men?" he asked.

"We want to join where we shall see some fighting," we said. "We don't want to go to the Pals or the Territorials."

His eyes opened wide.

"I've been waiting for you two chaps for days," he said. "I've got just the place for you."

In no time at all we were taking a medical examination. At this time the army still demanded a high standard of physical development and fitness. I had been a great walker. In those days we didn't talk about "hiking". We walked and we didn't need special clothes for the job. Some men still wore Norfolk suits for leisure and

The *Bull's Head Hotel* off the Old Market Place as it stood in the 1890s. In this Hotel Prince Charles made his headquarters when he marched with his Highlanders into Manchester in 1745.

"Oldest licensed house in Great Britain", the old *Seven Stars* in Withy Grove as it appeared in 1902. It did not live many years longer.

these were excellent for walking. I wasn't *that* well dressed but I spent many many hours and covered many many miles tramping over the Pennine moors. I tell you this so that you may understand that I thought I was reasonably fit.

"Can't you stand any straighter than that?" asked the doctor. My pride was suffering but I tried. "That's better," he said "You just about make it. Now the chest." I expanded for all I was worth. "Hum. You'll have to do better than that," he said. I breathed in so much air I wondered what *his* lungs must be using. "All right," he said. "I think you'll do."

Alas, my friend didn't pass the doctor. I was on my own.

And where did they send me but to a Special Reserve battalion of the Manchester Regiment. The Regiment had First and Second Battalions and additionally two Special Reserve battalions. The idea was that the Reserve units in peace time took in the volunteers who could be drafted later to join 'the regulars'. They trained for several weeks every year and received payment. Now they had been mobilised and were the 'feeders' for battalions on active service.

The officers and N.C.O.'s at the outset were regular soldiers. The rank and file were largely recruited from the not-so-wealthy quarters of Manchester — many from Ancoats or Angel Meadow.

To say that I went in at the deep end is an understatement. I had barely time to tell my parents what I had done when I was off with a draft to a night in the Manchesters' barracks at Ashton-under-Lyne. Sure enough this was no Pals Battalion. It was tough.

War has done so many dreadful things to so many people since that night I spent in Ashton that what happened to me may seem trivial.

The chief shock was that there I was away from home on my own two feet with an unknown future facing me. My civilian clothes went home in an untidy parcel and I went forward in a shoddy blue uniform — one of many rushed out by multiple tailoring firms to meet government demand. Youth is resilient and I got over the shock and somehow I managed to avoid being commissioned in the infantry so that I went to France as a Sergeant, was transferred compulsorily to the Royal Flying Corps and from there to the R.A.F. and came home in one piece and a little wiser but still with a great deal to learn.

No doubt my story of my experience will start many ex-servicemen remembering how they joined up. There were worse experiences than any which befell me.

I have given you the story in considerable detail because I want you to appreciate the irony, the bitter irony of fate.

The Pals Battalions, the very pick of the youth of the greater Manchester area went out to the Battle of the Somme. They climbed out of trenches and went forward in open order in the teeth of perfectly orientated machine-gun fire. A few of them lived. I joined one of their battalions when they went over at Arras later and they said that when their Colonel met the remnant of the battalion coming out he asked "What company is this?" They said he wept when they told him, "We are the battalion, Sir."

There were wonderful men of great academic and athletic promise in those battalions. By comparison I was something of a "softy". I never passed examinations. I had no competitive spirit. While they played lacrosse and rugby and soccer, I went tramping the moors, a solitary.

I felt pretty grim when I came home and looked round for my friends. There were some left, some of them damaged. I marvelled at the everlasting mercy which had brought me out alive. I believe my parents marvelled and were infinitely grateful. But the mercy didn't end there. Came a Second World War. This one found me "lobbying" in Manchester Town Hall. The representative for the rival newspaper group was James Holroyd who nowadays has a great reputation as an authority on Sherlock Holmes!

Kersal Cell, home of the family of John Byrom, who also invented a system of shorthand on which some modern methods are founded.

Together we witnessed and reported on a colossal phenomenon. It was the impact of war on that town hall. There were queues — long queues. On one side came men and women with strange un-English names. They had come to England after Poland was carved up between the European powers. They had come from Russian Poland and they had allowed themselves to be recorded as Russians. Now Russia was in pact with Germany and Poland was being invaded by Russians and Germans. These people were anxious to put the record straight. They wanted to be known as Poles.

On the other side came women — thousands and thousands of women to join the Womens' Voluntary Service for Civil Defence, which was being formed.

There were thousands and thousands of women and almost all of them wanted to drive vehicles. How the shape of things to come was varied is a long story not to be told here. It was a different W.V.S. from the original town hall concept which ultimately emerged.

My story is that after marvelling at what we had seen Jim Holroyd and I, by our own and devious ways and very much as a fortune of war, both progressed into the Government information services. Here was a war with a different flavour. I was observing Manchester at war on the home front.

On the first of October 1940 I left my office in the city and travelled four miles to my home for a meal. Eventually I switched on the radio and listened to the nine o'clock news. Sirens went but we were not terribly impressed, my wife and I. I was standing in characteristic male attitude before the fire. I heard a German aircraft somewhere overhead.

"That chap's making a run in — come on quick," I said to my wife.

Now we could hear anti-aircraft fire. With unhurried nerve the enemy made a trial run, turned back and running in again dropped one — two bombs. We never heard the third bomb. It hit the house.

We had dived into a cupboard under the staircase. Now we heard the place crashing down above us. Luckily the staircase held. Soon we heard voices. Civil Defence coming to find us and dig us out. It took a long time. We had minor scratches and we were very dirty and homeless and owned just what we stood up up in.

So far as I am concerned — and many others — Manchester has seen as much of warfare as is good for anyone.

There is no longer a Manchester Regiment.

And of course the Luftwaffe had a much better sense of direction than the Zeppelin skipper. I remember sitting at lunch in the canteen on the top floor of the *Manchester Guardian* building watching a cheeky German bomber flying at little more than roof top height over Market Street in broad daylight.

I hope Manchester may now say "Farewell to arms."

Under the eye of the law—suffragettes on parade in 1913—among them Annie Briggs, Evelyn Manesta and Lillian Forrester.

CHAPTER FOURTEEN

A Hole in the Head?

INEVITABLY someone is sure to ask how it is possible to write so much about Manchester without mentioning those great football teams Manchester City and Manchester United. My answer is that so often I have been hard at work in other branches of the news field when teams have been playing or results have been arriving that I could never find myself to be a 'follower'.

As a junior reporter I wrote about cricket and rugby for *The Umpire,* the paper which became the *Empire News,* and for the *Football Field,* a pink edition of the *Bolton Evening News.* I had played rugby at school and my cricket was the Saturday afternoon brand. These were activities which added shillings to my small income as a junior.

When I graduated to fully-fledged status opportunity directed my activities away from sport. It may be that as a consequence of years of compulsory indifference I have developed a hole in the head where sport ought to have its place. I hope not.

To those who have a keen interest in sport it is extremely important that they should know the results of the day's fixtures with as little delay as possible. This attitude of impatience has been encouraged by competition between newspapers in towns, particularly on Saturdays. The outcome is a hectic orgy of speed in those departments of newspaper production which get results on to paper in print.

In those years when Manchester had two evening papers blood pressures and temperatures could run very high around the tables where sports sub-editors worked. Not that papers can sacrifice speed today. The broadcasting services tread too closely on their heels.

It is well within my lifetime that pigeons have been used to carry reports of sporting occasions to newspaper offices. The practice was to send a copy boy with a basket of homing pigeons to the venue of an event. The reporter recording the occasion would write his report on pages of a special flimsy tissue which the boy would fold, and fasten to a leg of a pigeon with an elastic band. The pigeon was then sent into the air to find its way to a loft on the roof of the newspaper office.

"Those dark satanic mills"—an old cotton mill which stood in Newton Street.

Football! Buses load up here for the Manchester City ground at Maine Road.

Many people believe that homing pigeons only "home" because they are hungry. I have been told that it was a wicked and not unknown practice of pigeon carrying copy boys to put big handfuls of food, surreptitiously of course, into the pigeon baskets of boys from the rival paper. The result was that birds fed in this way would perch on the roof of a football stand and loiter there to watch the game instead of "homing".

A very early football memory of mine is of being in a railway train with my father passing through Ardwick. We heard a strange varying roar of human voices.

"We are passing Hyde Road," said my father. "That is the noise of the City crowd."

The City ground in those days was on a triangle of land wedged between diverging railway lines — main lines at that and very busy ones. If the players were not pursued by the roar of the crowd at any moment they might feel themselves urged on by the hurried snorting of main line locomotives of at least three vintages.

Before I became really aware of their greatness Manchester City had moved to Maine Road and their old ground had become a graveyard for Manchester Corporation's worn out public service vehicles. At one period I lived for a few years in exile at Glossop and from passing trains now and again I saw the last sad remains of a noble bus being consigned to the flames of a bonfire. I was relieved and grateful to be assured that it was not expected that the driver and conductor would commit suttee!

I can say though without any pride that I have trodden the hallowed turf of the Manchester United ground at Old Trafford. Believe it or not a match had been arranged between teams from the *Daily Mail* and the *Daily Express*. Football talent sprouts in unexpected places and men of promise were called from the profound recesses of the two great Manchester newspaper offices.

Of course it was essential that the match should be played in a morning. Daily newspaper people tend to rise late from their beds because most of them work late at night. In consequence their faculties are apt to be at their highest degree of efficiency after lunch.

It was a great privilege that we should be allowed the use of the United ground for such an event. That might well have been acknowledged round the bar of the Press Club any evening but the men in the teams which trooped out into a rather damp cool morning on a pitch where the going was, for amateurs, a little on the heavy side, did not express any great gratitude.

The scoring was frequent. I am not going to say which team won. Let that part of the story be lost in the limbo of forgotten debacles. Fortunately United hospitality included use of the hot baths and so the men who emerged after the match were acceptable in public houses.

The general feeling was one of thankfulness that a man does not need to be a first class footballer to be able to write about the game. The truth cannot be escaped that within a very short time afterwards the matter had been forgotten by the men who ceased to remember rivalries at the bar of a public house near the ground.

It was my lot to be Chairman of the Manchester Branch of the National Union of Journalists in 1958-59 and it was during my period of office that the Manchester United team, probably the greatest team that football has ever known, was decimated by an air disaster at Munich.

No need to recall the details of the smash. What I knew of it was that I became involved in the arguments about compensation and about insurance cover for journalists who fly. I have known a photographer who flew many scores of times usually in 'open-top' light aircraft taking pictures from the air and never worrying about insurance. Luckily nothing ever went amiss.

From the Munich crash however one learned that hardly any two of the journalists in the plane had the same kind of coverage. Not unnaturally there was criticism of much of the coverage. After such a loss it is human to feel that no compensation is adequate.

Junior reporters on local papers in my early days were privileged to attend most of the local funerals. I had that very doubtful privilege and found myself inured to the sight of sadness and mourning. That is not to say that one loses all human sympathy but obviously those officiating in any capacity on these occasions must retain their composure.

Sadly my composure suffered when I had to attend the funerals of the men who died at Munich and the memorial services which followed. It was a devastating experience and it began when I went to buy an evening newspaper from a girl who sold them at the front door of the *Daily Mail* building in Deansgate. She had just received a bundle of copies of the latest edition of the paper and as she looked at the front page she burst into tears. Until I saw what she had been reading I wondered why I should find myself standing on a busy sidewalk offering to buy a paper from a sobbing woman.

"They are gone!" she cried, "United are killed in an air smash!"

She spoke the prelude to an experience no man could live through with any joy. I am glad it was my chance to do something, however little, for the men who survived the crash.

Ancient buildings in Long Millgate, Manchester as they appeared in 1907—all swept away in the "march of progress".

CHAPTER FIFTEEN

Manchester Alphabet

THE man who drew the pictures and wrote the verses which compose the *Manchester Alphabet* had qualities which should have made him forever remembered by this city of his adoption. Unfortunately he died in 1916 — during the war in which the flower of my generation was being slaughtered.

In 1917 his widow gathered together some of his thoughts which were published privately under the title *The Art of Englishmen and other Writings of Roger Oldham.* In this slender book is biographical appreciation written by I. H. Swallow, a close friend of the Oldhams. This contribution tells us that Roger Oldham was born on February 9th, 1871 at Lincoln, the fourth of a family of six sons and one daughter. When he was three years of age the family moved to Sale, on Cheshire's southern fringe of Manchester.

With the exception of five years spent in London the rest of his life was passed in Manchester and district. However, he maintained an interest in his birthplace which was strengthened by his marriage.

He was sent to Manchester Grammar School which at that time had a reputation for bringing out the qualities of its boys. He did well there and left in 1887 at the age of sixteen. He was then articled to Charles Heathcote, a Manchester architect, in whose office he stayed from 1887 to 1891. Then he went to London for five years.

Chiefly it appears he studied at the Royal Academy. In 1896 he returned to Manchester and opened an office as an architect. It was noted that his office was also a studio where creative work was always going on. In 1903 a collection of his work was published under the title *Picturesque Cheshire.*

In 1906 his *Manchester Alphabet* was published.

He had married in 1904 Dorothy, second daughter of Charles Scorer of Lincoln. It must have been a very happy marriage and Roger Oldham a very lovable character. He was a devoted Christian with idealist views on the importance of art in the best kind of life. He took great interest in Sunday School work and in boys' clubs. He gave talks to various adult organisations and these talks have been described as in reality lay sermons.

He lectured to the Manchester Society of Architects. My father, James D. Mould, was an architect and a member of the Society and they were friends. Indeed my father had great respect for Roger Oldham and his skills and beliefs.

From Mr. Swallow's tribute one learns that Roger Oldham was deeply interested in the work of Ruskin, Moores, Browning, and Newbolt and other much read and discussed writers of the century he knew as a young man.

I have my father's copy of the *Manchester Alphabet* which Roger Oldham autographed with a thumb-nail sketch of himself at his desk and the signature "Roger Oldham, del pro J.D.M."

To people of my generation and some of later vintage the verses and pictures in Roger Oldham's *Manchester Alphabet* are powerfully nostalgic. For those lucky enough to be younger I felt it would be well to provide my own comments as I turn the pages and recall the past.

A for ANCOATS.

Of course a whole chapter could be written on this subject. No longer is it full of smoke and fogs. It gets its share of fog which isn't very much, but then Manchester was *the* pioneer city in Britain in smoke abatement and smokeless zones. And much of the smoke creating industry has gone from the area. No longer do the lasses wear shawls and clogs.

The evidence in the initial picture is all of the poverty of Ancoats — ill-fitting and patched clothing — the dominating symbol of the pawn shop.

There is a barge on the Rochdale canal, much of which is now filled in, and there is not a motor vehicle in sight.

No longer is it imperative that policemen should patrol in pairs in Ancoats. Slum clearance has been effective. But for long after the First World War Ancoats was a volatile locality. Friends of mine kept a fish and chip shop at New Cross, which is part of Ancoats really, and they found that life was never dull after 10.30 p.m. on a Saturday evening.

In the area behind Ancoats Lane, now Great Ancoats Street, there grew up over many years a vivid Italian colony. The inhabitants were chiefly in the itinerant ice-cream business. They were a very long way from Italy and the evolution of Mussolini. But came the Second World War and they were rounded up and packed into a ship which "set sail" for Canada but never arrived. Manchester still has an Italian colony and its members still love Manchester.

B for BOWDON.

The choice for "B" might have been Bridgewater, for that is the great Duke's Canal in which men are fishing in the picture.

Manchester and Liverpool are the great Lancashire cities but they both balance on the edge of Cheshire. Bowdon and its adjacent Altrincham are in Cheshire. The Duke of Bridgewater was an eighteenth century dandy. No waistcoats more flowered than those he wore. But he was disappointed in love and in his unhappiness he remembered Lancashire and Cheshire. He came north and somehow he found an engineering genius called Brindley — illiterate but brilliant. He had coal mines at Worsley and he linked them by canal with Liverpool. Brindley knew how to puddle clay to make a canal hold water.

But what about the railway? Well of course when steam was developed the easy way to penetrate south was to follow the straight line of the canal over the flat Cheshire land. As Manchester grew and the cotton towns grew, little railway companies multiplied.

Never forget of course that the first passenger railway station in the world was opened in Manchester.

But the C.L.C. or M.S.J. and A.R. — what were they? The Manchester South Junction and Altrincham Railway was the company which ran out to Altrincham and opened up a dormitory area in Cheshire which became very fashionable and popular. The Cheshire Lines Committee was a pioneer effort to bring order from chaos by having one management for a tangle of permanent way ownership to the south of Manchester.

C for CHORLTON.

Chorlton — well, Manchester has two Chorltons. Early in its expansionist history the developing town swallowed a little neighbour called Chorlton-on-Medlock. It had been known as Chorlton Row and then became a township with a Town Hall and a council of sorts. As my generation met it, it was densely populated working class and you passed through it on the way home of an evening. Well, that isn't the Chorlton Roger Oldham chose to typify the letter "C".

His Chorlton is Chorlton-cum-Hardy and as you can see it had, and has, trees and a church yard and suburban atmosphere. Unkind people regarded its dormitory growth as pretentious. It still has atmosphere. When Manchester people talk about Chorlton this is the one they usually mean. A colleague of mine on the editorial staff of an evening paper was sent out by our news editor to search for Hardy. Except in postal addresses people tend to forget the double barrelled tag. I knew where to find Hardy!

A for ANCOATS

A dreary place is Ancoats,
'Tis full of smoke and fogs,
The lasses wear shawls on their heads
Their feet are shod with clogs.
'Tis really not a pleasant place
Upon a rainy day ;
We have to start with Ancoats tho',
For Ancoats starts with A.

D for DALTON

John Dalton lived in Manchester
A hundred years ago,
A famous scientific man
As all the world doth know.
He's fishing now in our Town Hall
In stagnant H_2O.

G for "GUARDIAN"

" The Guardian " is a candid friend
And guide to sundry persons,
It compliments the very good
And scarifies the worse 'uns.

B for BOWDON

The men who sleep in Bowdon
In Manchester by day are,
They travel by the C.L.C.
Or M.S.J. & A.R.

C for CHORLTON

Chorlton's in the suburbs,
The Houses there have gates,
And people come in winter time,
If frosty, with their skates.

E for EXCHANGE

Royal Exchange has a very big floor
It's not big enough, so they open the door
come out in the street, do merchants galore.

F for FRESCO

Historical scenes of Manchester town
Were painted in fresco by Ford Madox Brown.
A fresco is something that can't run away
It's stuck on the plaster for ever and aye.

H for HEATON PARK

Let children come
From dreary slum
And din of dusty highways,
And once a week
Play hide and seek
In nature's leafy by-ways.

I for IRWELL

I is for IRWELL
for IRK
and for INK,
But none of these Liquids
Is wholesome to drink.

It was a December evening but a mild one and my girl friend and I went walking down a country lane deep in serious conversation. We came to a farm and under a light by a big barn door we stopped and I proposed marriage! I must have had considerable nerve because I had the engagement ring in a box in my pocket! Very luckily for me I was accepted and so could produce the ring. It was not Hardy who did the kissing though the barn door was part of Hardy's Farm.

D for DALTON.

Manchester has always done less than justice to John Dalton. He was a great scientist. He did much pioneer experimentation. For example he made the early tentative steps towards the explosion of the atom. When he retired he received a very modest pension. The city has a street named after him which is being "developed" piecemeal.

In the great hall of the Town Hall he is shown in one of the murals stirring the mud at the bottom of a stagnant pool to cause the marsh gas to rise. His assistant, a small boy, is capturing the gas in an inverted jar. It's a good picture but in some ways a curious memorial to a great man. In the main entrance to the Town Hall is a statue of Dalton which gives him greater dignity.

E for EXCHANGE.

Now what profound nostalgia is aroused by the picture of Manchester Royal Exchange! Oh yes, it is still there though vastly altered and no one seems to know quite what to do with it. It was a cotton exchange and at its "greatest" had the biggest exchange floor in the world.

I can remember when it had that magnificent pillared portico and wide staircase and the open-topped electric trams passed there as the horse trams had done in an earlier day. The crowd in the street and on the staircase in the picture is no exaggeration. In the hours coming up to High Change on Tuesday the floor was too small. They doubled the size of it later. And look at those tall silk hats! Hats were always worn in the Exchange and long ago they were all tall hats. A firm of cotton brokers having offices near the Exchange kept a rack of shiny head gear ready so that representatives dashing out to do business "on the floor" could be suitably crowned.

The cotton trade changed its shape and its size and its habits. The telephone, imports from developing countries, man-made fibres, plastics, all played a part.

F for FRESCO.

It was realised after Ford Madox Brown had painted several pictures on the plaster that it could be wiser to have the remaining pictures done on canvas. As you walk round the great hall of Manchester Town Hall you cannot easily detect which pictures are on the plaster "for ever and aye". They are all looked after very carefully.

I don't know whether the portrait of the painter seen here is accurate. In his day long hair and whiskers were badges of artistic occupation. The picture on which he is seen to be engaged is the one showing the expulsion of the Danes from Manchester. Clearly they must have been a trial to merit such rough treatment as the picture in the Town Hall shows.

G for GUARDIAN.

In 1906 when the *Manchester Alphabet* was published the *Manchester Guardian* was beginning to reap the reward of courage and determination.

It was not one of the oldest newspapers in the country but it was a paper which had "hit the headlines" outside its own circulation area. This odd publicity was achieved because the editor, proprietor Charles Prestwich Scott, was "agin" the war in South Africa. The paper told its readers that Britain was engaging in an unworthy campaign.

Confronting the shouters and flag wavers it was a vastly unpopular line to take. But the *Manchester Guardian* went on living. If you can manage to sustain a swim against the tide for long enough the time will come when the current is going your way. By 1906 the dust had settled on the veldt and people could begin to see what kind of victory we had achieved.

Observe that the paper was referred to as *The Guardian* although it was not able to eliminate the "Manchester" from its title for many years thereafter. The paper is shown displayed as it is still to be found on a rack in the older Manchester clubs. There is no prize for identifying the political characters whose portraits appear.

H for HEATON PARK.

I have spent many hours there. I could drive in and park my car near the Hall at a point from which I looked out over the parklands. The graceful eighteenth century Hall was an ancestral home of the Earls of Wilton. It was bought in the century by Manchester Corporation and since then has been much used and mis-used.

In the First World War it was a camp site and training ground for the "Pals" battalions of the Manchester Regiment. In the Second World War the R.A.F. took it over.

I don't know exactly at what point in history the peacocks vanished from its lawns. I remember them. I remember also the multi-coloured rabbits in the netting-enclosed copse behind the hall. When families lost interest in their pet rabbits or found them too prolific they popped them over the wire. It was allowed, and the rabbits could not stray to damage gardens. In the Second War the rabbits vanished. Very sinister.

I for IRWELL.

It is no exaggeration to say that the Irwell is probably the hardest worked river in Europe or maybe in the world — for its length. In its thirty miles its waters have been used for various cooling processes and more important it has received pollution of great variety. The Irk is a tributary flowing through Manchester and suffering its own burden of use.

The picture shows the Irwell flowing between the cities of Manchester and Salford — a natural and time-honoured boundary. In 1906 there were small vessels on the river — some carrying sightseers!

The buildings seen on the banks are disappearing or have disappeared and taller giants take their places. There in the background is the tower of the "Owd Church" — now the Cathedral.

J for JOULE.

Now here is the statue of "The man with the mousetrap" as the irreverent are wont to describe it. Records tell me that J. P. Joule was one of the greatest of English physicists. His statue faces that of the other great physicist, Dalton. Joule determined the mechanical equivalent of heat and researched on electro-magnetism. But the achievement which put him into Manchester Town Hall was the development of the jacquard system of weaving.

The punching of holes in a sheet or roll of paper is used today for the recording of all kinds of information. In jacquard weaving the design to be woven into the cloth is recorded on a loop of paper which goes round and round repeating its story on yard after yard of cloth.

K for KING STREET.

There are still cake shops in and around King Street but what a pleasure it is to look up that street and see so little traffic about! Its great problem today is the parking of motor cars. Of course its upper end — up the hill which faces you in the picture — has acquired many modern buildings on the left hand side. For the enlightenment of the visitor it should be explained that King Street is to the old Mancunian what Bond Street is to the man who knows and loves his London.

L for LORD MAYOR.

The view seen through the main entrance of the Town Hall has changed little. It is true that the canopy of the memorial to Prince Albert has lost many of its ornamentations through erosion and its removal is recommended. But the buildings across the square are untouched. It would be sensational today of course if distinguished visitors arrived in a horse-drawn vehicle. The point about this picture is that the Lord Mayor is standing at his front door!

Manchester is one of the very few cities which provide the Lord Mayor with a residence inside the Town Hall during his term of office. I have been fortunate enough to be entertained many times in those very comfortable quarters.

M for MOTOR CAR.

And now the motor car and in the background the old *Seven Stars* public house — demolished many years ago alas! It *has* been claimed that it was the oldest licensed house in the north — perhaps in the country. It was every bit genuine and well worthy of preservation. The "modern mammoth Midland" is the *Midland Hotel* and I hope I shall be forgiven for saying that it is now a period piece in its own right.

N for "N".

Motor car registration was new and important in 1906 but the marking on the car in the picture does not conform to the regulations regarding size and type of letters and figures as we know them today. Perhaps that is the transgression of which the policeman is making a note. Today a car with a solitary letter "N" in its registration is likely to have vintage value.

O for OWL.

Ulula (the Owl) — that was the name of our Grammar School magazine. The owl was on the cover. On my cap was a silver owl of which I was very proud. I lived for years near a woodland which was a haunt of owls. When I worked on a national daily newspaper I came home often from a late turn in the early hours of the morning. As I came near home the owls greeted me. One morning through the gloom I saw one of them drop like a stone onto a garden lawn where a mouse or some other unfortunate small creature was moving.

J for JOULE

Just peep inside the Town Hall door
And there you will espy
An old man in his dressing gown
Who looks with stony eye
At something he holds in his hand,
I do not quite know why.

M for MOTOR CAR

The face and pace of Manchester
Have many changes seen,
From the grass of Angel Meadow
And the blades of Ardwick Green;
From the Pack Horse and the Pillion
And " the ancient Seven Stars,"
To the modern mammoth Midland
And the monstrous Motor Cars.

P for PICTURE GALLERY

Go up some steps in Mosley Street
And through a sculpture hall,
Climb up some further flights of steps,
And thro' a turnstile crawl,
At last behold the pictures,
Hung up on every wall.

K for KING STREET

There's King Street
And there's King Street South
And also King Street West,
They each of them begin with K,
I know which I like best —
The one in which the cake shop is—
Let's go inside and rest.

L for LORD MAYOR

The Lord Mayor is a lovely sight
All in his coat of red,
A golden chain about his neck,
A big hat on his head ;
He entertains the city's guests
And sees that they are fed.

N

w these monstrous Motor Cars,
product of the age,
has only just been mentioned
the last preceding page)
re a letter put behind them
signify to men
place which they belong to,
us :—Manchester is N.

O for OWL

The Grammar School Owl,
That very wise fowl,
Was the crest of the pious Hugh Oldham,
Who made it a rule
When he founded the School
That the boys should do always what's
told 'em.

Q for De QUINCEY

e Quincey once lived at a place called
Greenhey
hich *was* a green place in T. Quincey's
day.

R for ROBERT

This monument so stately
To the late Sir Robert Peel,
Is the guardian of our traffic
And the public commonweal.

In Heaton Park the owls were fond of roosting on the roof of the Hall. These birds have peculiar habits. They eat the whole of a mouse and then regurgitate the bones and hair and skin in a neat ball which falls to the ground and gives a clue to the owl's roosting place.

P for PICTURE GALLERY.

Manchester never has enough room to display its enormous art collection. The Art Gallery in Mosley Street is a fine old building and it would be heartbreaking if it disappeared. Of course it was not built as an Art Gallery. It was one of the Mechanics Institute buildings erected during the wave of nineteenth century enthusiasm for such ventures — the period when Warrington was known as the Athens of the North.

If you look at the top of the picture you will see a corner of the bas reliefs which fringe the roof lighting. They are a good reproduction of the Elgin Marbles. The entrance to "Picture Gallery" seen here is just as it stands today — undamaged after another sixty-five years.

Q for DE QUINCEY.

I have not been able to prove it but I believe the house shown in the "Q for de Quincey" picture was the boyhood home of the genius.

It stood in Greenheys and I don't suppose you will find many people who remember where Greenheys was — or even that there ever was a Greenheys. It lay close to the area which has become Manchester's academic complex — the University area. Roger Oldham erred, I am afraid, in calling the district Greenhey without the final "s". In the late nineteenth century Manchester's big "German Colony" took possession of Greenheys.

R for ROBERT.

In choosing Robert — the "bobby" to illustrate the letter "R" he gave us a wealth of Manchester history. The policeman he illustrates is the constable with red hair and whiskers known to passers by as "Rufus" who did point duty in Manchester for many years. I remember seeing him on the Corporation Street — Market Street crossing.

It seems incredible that we have with us now generations which know nothing of the string of point duty policemen in the main streets of Manchester.

Rufus, a frock coated policeman with no collar and tie showing and standing in the straw which was thoughtfully provided to keep his feet warm and dry on the stone-paved streets is shown on duty at the top of Mosley Street, his back being to St Peter's Church which disappeared many years ago.

The Church was on an island site in what is now St Peter's Square and the city war memorial shares the island with a cross commemorating the church and minuscule park — chiefly a refuge of stone benches much used as a haven on warm and sunny days.

On the rank by the church there is in the picture a hansom cab — the cabby leans over as if he is asleep. Behind the church with flags flying from turrets is the *Midland Hotel.*

S for SHUDEHILL.

At a time when there are plans to move Covent Garden Market from the centre of London it is appropriate to have a souvenir of Shudehill which is Manchester's traditional wholesale fruit and vegetable market. What can be seen in the drawing of the open-sided market in the background is just as it stands today. But like Covent Garden it is to be moved away from the city centre. Its official title is Smithfield Market and Shudehill is really the name of the thoroughfare which runs up one side of it, but when Mancunians talk about the Market they call it Shudehill.

T for TRAMS.

There was no "queueing" in 1906. It was the First World War that taught people to "stand in line" as they say in the United States. This was the day of tramcars with unsheltered upper storeys. There were notices advising passengers not to touch the overhead wires. It was also the day when running a tramway system was a profitable business.

Look behind the stout gentleman in the very loud check suit on the right of the picture and there by the cord which hangs down from the overhead trolley you see a trolley boy. These boys were for many years a feature of Manchester tramway service. It was held to be impossible for a conductor to collect fares up-stairs and down and to keep an eye on the trolley. So these boys in smart uniforms rode on the after deck of the tram and controlled the trolley.

During a period between the wars when short skirts were fashionable the boys were suspected of too keen an interest in the legs of the ladies who climbed to the tops of the trams. They, the boys, disappeared from the trams soon afterwards.

U for UMPIRE.

No Manchester anthology of any kind would be complete without some reference to Old Trafford county cricket ground.

S for SHUDEHILL

Heaps of oranges and apples,
Piles of "tates" and curly greens,
Bananas, sprouts, and artichokes,
Late peas and early beans,
Inside a great glass market
Is what Shudehill really means.

V for VICTORIA

A model of nobility
To all of every station,
Victoria the well-beloved
The mother of the nation.

Y for YARN

To business men in Manchester
The Yarn is daily bread,
They talk of hanks and mules and counts,
And throstle-frames and thread,
As did their grandsires long ago
Who now, of course, are dead.

T for TRAMS

Tram Cars glide about the streets
If they were alive,
men and women fight for seats
night at half past five.

U for UMPIRE

They keep men at Old Trafford
In snowy raiment clad,
To tell men when they are run out
And if the light is bad.

W for WHIT-WEEK WALK

The scholars' walk in Manchester
quite a pretty sight,
he boys all have their faces washed,
heir boots with blacking bright,
he girls all have their hair in curl,
heir dresses spotless white.

X for EXODUS

Each Saturday at 1 o'clock
The people leave the town en bloc,
But if you wait till 10 to 2
You'll only see a very few.

Z for ZOO

Belle Vue it is true
Is a very good Zoo,
Brass bands and rip-raps
And set pieces too,
Are part of the programme
At Manchester Zoo.

Roger Oldham.
del. pro
J·D·M.

The autographed thumb-nail
sketch on my father's copy.

Here is a good picture of the stand with a test match crowd of spectators. Though they don't care to mention it, Manchester men know that the cricket ground is not in Manchester. It is in the neighbouring borough of Stretford. So is the Manchester United Football ground and the Trafford Park industrial estate. Perhaps new schemes of local government will sort these things out.

V for VICTORIA.

It was believed that Queen Victoria had refused to come to Manchester to open the new Town Hall because the city had a statue of Oliver Cromwell. The city's loyalty never faltered. Manchester's statue on the broad pavement in Piccadilly is on a generous scale. It shows the old Queen with voluminous drapery. She sits enthroned and behind her — on the reverse of the chair back so to speak — are minor figures showing a woman with two infants in her arms. There is an inscription which says "Let me but hear your love and I will bear your cares."

I have understood and believed that the great Queen was petite. Dignified, yes, and of dominating character but perhaps today we should do her greater justice by not showing her so much more than life size.

W for WHIT-WEEK WALK.

Throughout the world there are some few religious festivals which are outstanding. Generally they have the form of a demonstration of faith which is vastly impressive whether you are a follower of the particular faith involved or not.

In Lancashire, Whitsuntide is the season when Christian men women and children of various denominations give witness of their faith by walking in procession. One has known these demonstrations to hold up traffic in Manchester for a whole week. I can remember when it was also impossible to do business not only in Whit-week but during the week before and the week afterwards.

The most spectacular processions have been always those organised by the Roman Catholics. Most recently in addition to the carrying of a flower-bedecked statue of the Madonna by the Italians there has been a Ukrainian contingent in national costume.

The various religious societies have paraded uniformly clad, the girls in blue or white or green. The banners carried bear religious pictures and names of churches from which they come.

The building in the background of the picture is the Art Gallery of course — just as we see it today.

X for EXODUS.

The Saturday exodus illustrated reminds us that it was in Manchester that the Saturday half holiday was invented. It was usual to give office and warehouse staffs a half day during the week but on Saturdays most of them worked very late. No task must be left over to Monday. It was chiefly through the campaigning of young men on office staffs that a uniform Saturday half day was agreed. They spread rumours that certain firms were going to make the change and behold! It happened. There was much trade rivalry and no firm wanted to be the one left out.

The homeward rush is shown in Oxford Street. In the distance are the *Princes Restaurant,* no longer there, and St Peter's Church, which I never saw though it was there when I was very young.

Y for YARN.

The grandsires seen talking about yarn are not likely to have talked of mules and throstle frames. Theirs would be the day of handloom weaving — the day when spinning was a domestic occupation just as knitting is so often today. The great days of the throstle frame and the mule came with the development of steam, of mechanisation and of "dark satanic mills". They were adjuncts of the production of yarn by factory methods. The throstle was given its name because the bobbins on which it wound yarn made a whistling noise like a bird.

Yarn is, of course, thread and in the eighteenth century which this picture invokes it was woollen thread everywhere. The advent of American cotton sent the woollen industry over the Pennines into Yorkshire.

The half-timbered building which is the background to this picture is identifiable as having existed in Long Millgate until late in the nineteenth century.

Z for ZOO.

The history of Belle Vue Zoo is a wonderful story. It is the story of the Jennison family who turned a farm some distance from the growing town of Manchester into a mighty pleasure resort, the nucleus of which was the zoological collection. The town has grown out to the zoo; surrounded it, and left it still a very active pleasure precinct as near the city centre as only the internal combustion engine could make it.

Once on a time the Jennison's brewed beer, made bread and meat pies, printed tickets and posters, in fact created a self-contained pleasure town within the brick boundary walls of Belle Vue.

Mammoth firework displays were a feature of the programme. Fireworks were once made for the set pieces which were built on an island in a small lake. In the picture the island can be just seen with a woodland setting upon it and pleasure boats before it.

These displays usually had as subject great British victories or shall we say achievements, as for example the relief of Lucknow or Ladysmith. Scenes in which elephants could be used to give authenticity were very popular. I don't think there was ever an elephant quite as big as the one in the picture. Belle Vue Zoo is still a good zoo.

Where they shopped on wet days. The Deansgate Arcade which was demolished to make way for a Co-operative departmental store.

CHAPTER SIXTEEN

Envoi

MANCHESTER is changing. Of course it is. It's a continuing process. Cities and towns are like other structures of human organisation, they are always changing. Nothing stands still. If a city does not move forward boldly into the future it slips back towards decay.

As much as any city Manchester has a special urgency in moving forward. Its history shows a curious tendency to lose ground through no fault in its outlook. It could have died with the cotton industry — but it didn't. Bravely it became a great engineering centre.

In the 1890s its future was threatened but men of enterprise gave it a shot in the arm by opening the Ship Canal. Earlier the Manchester and Liverpool Quakers had injected new vigour by opening the Liverpool and Manchester Railway. Earlier still the great Duke of Bridgewater shook it up by opening his Manchester Liverpool canal. Now it appears that the Ship Canal flourishes and the great modern airport at Ringway puts the city in the front rank of commercial centres.

The great immediate problem is one which afflicts the whole country — the inadequacy of roads. I once wrote a series of newspaper articles on the roads out of Manchester. They radiate like the spokes of a wheel. Each road had an individuality. Much of the character of those highways has disappeared — torn down, swept away by road improvements, slum clearance, property development.

Perhaps someday someone will dig my highway saga from the files. They will exclaim in astonishment no doubt at the roads I described. But let me reveal that when I wrote I had before me a far earlier series of articles on the same roads written by the Lancashire dialect poet Edwin Waugh. There was far more character in the roads in his day than in mine.

It made such a difference when traffic moved slowly enough for people to be able to look around them. It made a great difference when a vehicle could pull up at the roadside anywhere without worry about double yellow lines. To drive along the roads in and out of Manchester today demands intense concentration on the job. Enormous transport vehicles thunder along with you or pass in the opposite direction.

As you will have gathered I spent my young life in a small locality north of Manchester. Between five and six o'clock in the morning great heavy open lorries on steel-tyred wheels came trundling past. They were drawn by beautiful Shire horses at a steady walking pace. The drivers had their stopping places. In those days the 'carters' pubs' were open at 5.00 a.m. These pubs were strategically placed half way up any hill. They demanded a breather for the horses. There were horse troughs or buckets and open air taps. The horse had a drink. So did the carter.

These lorries were bringing in the grey cloth 'lumps' or rolls from the mills of East Lancashire. They would be in Manchester between eight and nine o'clock and once the lorry was backed into a loading and unloading bay of a warehouse the carter could go for a drink and to eat his sandwiches.

For the uninitiated I must explain a peculiarity of the cotton industry. Whatever may happen today, and of course organisation *is* quite different — the man who produced the grey cloth knew nothing of its ultimate fate and destination. Grey cloth is and was an unpatterned raw material for the printer or dyer. It went out to India in great quantities. It was dyed in surrealist native patterns for African markets.

On the face of it, it should be desperately simple to produce a saleable grey cloth. There were enterprising firms which spent much money trying to produce it, and failed.

We can laugh now but there was much anxiety in those days of the slow moving lorry loads about the mad passion for speed! The bicycle was enjoying

New Cross—the beginning of Oldham Road—at the end of the nineteenth century—horse omnibuses, a barefoot newsboy, a horse trough in the middle of the road.

St James' Hall stood where the Calico Printers building now stands. The Hall is pictured here with a horse-drawn double decker tram going by in about 1890.

its peak popularity. People were fined daily in the magistrates' courts for 'scorching'. All you had to do was put your head down over the handlebars and ride for all you were worth and on the word of an observing policeman you stood convicted.

All I try to show is the immense change which has taken place in the life of a city in one short lifetime. It is consciousness of this rapidly changing picture which has urged me to set down what I remember of this my city. It *is* only what one man remembers. It is *not* a detailed report of a research. It is a yielding to nostalgia. I hope it will stimulate many others to remember and fill in some of the gaps.

There is of course one story which pleads to be written very fully and with much careful research — the story of the old Manchester Assize Courts at Strangeways. What famous trials took place there! It was my fortune, good or bad according to how you look at these things, to attend many of them as a newspaper reporter.

One very hectic night enemy raiders destroyed the old buildings and much property round them including the Woolsack, the pub where many of the various people interested in the law's operation met to eat fine roast beef and drink well-kept ale.

The Assize Court buildings were in many ways strange when compared with the new Law Courts in the centre of the city. The great entrance hall had a magnificent hammer beam roof. The entrance was up a splendid flight of steps at the top of which the trumpeters stood to herald the arrival of the Judges. The Assize Courts building and the adjacent County Police Court, which survives, were on an 'island'.

They were all county territory with County Police jurisdiction, inside the City Police area. On the front of the Assize building were standards of measurement — they were brass — and I have heard a retired policeman tell how in serving at the police station on the site he had the job of polishing these long strips of metal — the yard among them of course.

A strange feature was that on a tower on the building was a statue — Moses writing on a tablet of stone. He was writing with his left hand! After the night of disaster the ruins remained for a time and then were dismantled. I have heard it said that when Moses was brought down from his lofty perch his left hand with the pen disappeared!

At last there remained a public car park where once justice had been liberally dispensed.

The tumult and the shouting dies.

Tib Street, Manchester, so called because it follows the course of the submerged River Tib, has long been famous as a market for pets.

REELER. HOT-WATER WOMAN. HAND-MULE SPINNER. WINDER. OVERLOOKER TO SELF-AC

KNOCKER-UP.   HALF-TIMER.   SCAVENGER.   THROSTLE

THE COTTON FAMINE: GROUP OF M